AFRICAN-AMERICANS

AFRICAN-AMERICANS

Essential Perspectives

Edited by Wornie L. Reed

Prepared under the auspices of the
William Monroe Trotter Institute,
University of Massachusetts at Boston
Wornie L. Reed, General Editor

AH

Auburn House
Westport, Connecticut • London

Library of Congress Cataloging-in-Publication Data

African-Americans : essential perspectives / edited by Wornie L. Reed.
p. cm.
"Prepared under the auspices of the William Monroe Trotter Institute, University of Masschusetts at Boston."
Includes bibliographical references and index.
ISBN 0–86569–221–1 (alk. paper). — ISBN 0–86569–222–X (pbk. : alk. paper)
1. Afro-Americans—Social conditions—1975– 2. Afro-Americans—Economic conditions. 3. Afro-Americans—Politics and government. 4. Justice, Administration of—United States. I. Reed, Wornie L. II. William Monroe Trotter Institute.
E185.86.A335 1993
305.896′073—dc20 92–31298

British Library Cataloguing in Publication Data is available.

Library of Congress Catalog Card Number: 92–31298
ISBN: 0–86569–221–1 (hc); 0–86569–222–X (pb)

First published in 1993

Auburn House, 88 Post Road West, Westport, CT 06881
An imprint of Greenwood Publishing Group, Inc.

Printed in the United States of America

The paper used in this book complies with the Permanent Paper Standard issued by the National Information Standards Organization (Z39.48–1984).

10 9 8 7 6 5 4 3 2 1

Contents

Tables

Preface

This volume is one of four books produced from the project "Assessment of the Status of African-Americans," coordinated by the William Monroe Trotter Institute at the University of Massachusetts at Boston. The studies from this project were the result of several developments, most notably the conflicting assessments of the status of African-Americans being reported in the 1980s and the controversy surrounding a study that was being conducted by the National Research Council. African-Americans are plagued by problems. These problems include unemployment, underemployment, poverty, crime, and poor health. The gap between blacks and whites in economic status is not closing. Consequently, there is a great need to examine trends, evaluate programs, and recommend social policies to address these problems. So in 1984, with $2 million in funding from foundations, the National Research Council (NRC) of the National Academy of Sciences began a study to report on the status of blacks from 1940 to the present and on the future status of blacks in the United States.

The NRC study, which was billed as an update of Gunnar Myrdal's study, *An American Dilemma*, faced severe criticisms along the way. Many critics complained about the limited involvement of African-American scholars in the conceptualization, planning, and development of the project. They noted that many African-Americans who are prominent in some of the areas under study were conspicuously omitted from the study panels.

Since the NRC study was intended as an update of the Myrdal study, it might be useful to review the Myrdal work. Gunnar Myrdal was recruited to direct that study from Sweden, a country with no history of colonization and no apparent vested interest in the history of black-white relations in the United States. The work, which was published in 1944, reigned for nearly a quarter of a century as the authoritative study of black life in the United States. There was no competing major study.

In a masterfully crafted argument, Myrdal concluded that the racial oppression of African-Americans was the result of an American conflict, an American dilemma: the discrepancy between an egalitarian ideology and racially discriminatory behavior. He addressed the real issue, racial oppression; however, he presented it in combination with a very positive statement about America—about the American Creed, thereby making his overall assessment of racial problems more palatable to his audience.

An American Dilemma became a classic within American social science, and it reached a broad readership. For two decades, it was the definitive survey of black Americans. Civil rights activists, ministers, teachers, and social workers used the book as a reference in their struggles against segregation.

In spite of its widespread influence in the African-American community as well as in the northern white community, the study had its black critics. Many questioned whether racism could be reduced by addressing the contradiction in America's conscience. On the other hand, liberal social scientists were reluctant to criticize a book that forcefully condemned racism and spread this message to a wide audience.

Some social scientists argued that Myrdal paid too little attention to institutional racism and that the elimination of racial discrimination and domination would require the addressing of social structural problems and institutional change. In a significant critique, the novelist Ralph Ellison applauded the book but situated the Myrdal study in a historical line of social science writings that had done more to maintain the status quo for African-Americans than to change it.

The African-American sociologist Oliver Cox was another prominent critic. He argued that in studying social problems, it was important to examine the relationship between social problems and social structure.

Critics of the NRC's study were concerned about the ramifications of a major study of African-Americans in the ideological climate of the 1980s. There had been a dismantling of the Great Society Programs and a cease-fire in the war on poverty. And some critics were concerned that a major study by a prestigious academic organization like the NRC might serve to validate the 1980s trends toward limiting the role of government in addressing the ills of society, especially those concerning race. Furthermore, these critics contended that the NRC study groups, while including a number of persons with commitment to principles of equality and fairness, included a significant number of scholars who rule out both the historical oppression of African-Americans and contemporary discrimination against blacks as major influences in the present condition of African-American communities.

As a result of these concerns and considerations, in the spring of 1987, I initiated the project "The Assessment of the Status of African-Americans" at the William Monroe Trotter Institute at the University of Massachusetts at Boston. Thirty-five scholars were organized into study groups, one for each of six topics: education; employment, income, and occupations; political participation and the administration of justice; social and cultural change; health status and medical care; and the family. The study groups were established to analyze the status of African-Americans in each of the topical areas in anticipation of the results and analyses of the National Research Council's Study Committee on the Status of Black Americans. We wanted to have the widest possible discussion of the present condition of African-Americans and the social policy implications of that condition.The multidisciplinary group of scholars comprising the study groups included persons from all sections of the country and from varied settings—private and public universities, historically black colleges and universities, and private agencies. Each of the study groups met and drafted an agenda for examining significant issues in its respective topical areas. Members chose issues from this agenda within their areas of expertise and identified scholars who had written extensively on other issues on the agenda. These other scholars, 26 in number, made a variety of contributions, including original papers, reprints, notes and materials, and/or substantial commentaries on draft documents from the study groups. Each of the study groups developed its own conclusions and policy recommendations. A list of these scholars by study group is given in the appendix.

Despite the pressures of time and limited financial support for this work, the studies were completed and released in six preliminary volumes by the William Monroe Trotter Institute. The final production of the studies has been done by Auburn House Publishers in four volumes: *The Education of African-Americans* (1991), *Research on the African-American Family: A Holistic Perspective* (1993), *Health and Medical Care of African-Americans* (1993), and *African-Americans: Essential Perspectives* (1993). In addition to study group members and other contributors, I am indebted to several individuals at the Trotter Institute for the production of this volume. Special thanks are offered to Linda Kluz and Suzanne Baker, production editors; and to Eva Hendricks and Gemima Remy, word processing operators. Special thanks are due also to John Harney of Auburn House Publishers for his encouragement and support for this work.

Wornie L. Reed

Introduction

This volume is an effort to describe and assess the current status of African-Americans by looking at several selected areas of African-American life. To get a picture of the directions of trends in these status indicators, data was examined over periods ranging from two to five decades. On most measures the situation of African-Americans has improved over the longer period of time. However, much of this improvement occurred in the 1960s following key U.S. Supreme Court decisions and federal legislative acts, especially *Brown v. Board of Education,* the Civil Rights Act of 1964, and the Voting Rights Act of 1965. Since the early 1970s, however, African-Americans have lost ground in comparison to whites in several areas, most notably in the realm of economics.

Poverty among blacks *and* whites increased during the 1980s. Some eight million more persons were poor in 1987 than a decade earlier. Two million of these new poor were blacks, blacks were three times as likely as whites to be poor, and nearly half of all black children lived in poverty (Jacobs, 1989).

These shocking trends cannot be attributed to single female–headed families, to the refusal of "lazy" blacks to work, or to generous welfare benefits that discourage work force participation. The facts simply tell us otherwise: Black poverty rates were higher in 1987 than they were a decade earlier, despite the fact that black unemployment rates were the same and the percentage of the black poor living in female-headed families was lower.

On all key measures the economic situation of black Americans continues to lag far behind that of white Americans. In 1986, the median income of black families was only 57.1% of that of white families. This was up only slightly from the 51.1% rate in 1947, and down from rates in the mid-1970s when black family income was occasionally as much as 60% of that of whites (Simms, 1988).

A majority of African-Americans in a 1987 survey identified unemployment as one of the three most important public policy issues facing the nation—and for good reason. By 1987 the nation's economy had been steadily expanding for five years, but the unemployment rate for blacks nationwide was 13%—almost two and one-half times the unemployment rate for whites (Simms, 1988).

Black unemployment rates have, on average, been approximately double the rates for whites since the end of World War II. Until the mid-1970s the ratio of black to white unemployment had tended to rise when the economy has expanded. Since 1976, however, the ratio has tended to rise rather than fall each time the economy expanded. In other words, the gap between black unemployment and white unemployment *increased* when the economy improved.

It may be useful to study disadvantaged individuals to address their plights. In this instance it is useful to study African-American communities and the individuals within those communities who constitute the negative statistics. This is appropriate. However, it is the orientation of this volume that it is necessary to study these individuals in context; in other words, in terms of their interactions with the institutions of American society. Such an approach may be considered a social systems analysis, where African-Americans and African-American families are seen as interacting with and being affected by major institutions of society (Billingsley, 1986).

Perhaps the following story of a physician trying to explain the dilemmas of the modern practice of medicine is illustrative of the importance of this approach:

"You know," he said, "sometimes it feels like this. There I am standing by the shore of a swiftly flowing river and I hear the cry of a drowning man. So I jump into the river, put my arms around him, pull him to shore and apply artificial respiration. Just when he begins to breathe, there is another cry for help. So I jump into the river, reach him, pull him to shore, apply artificial respiration, and then just as he begins to breathe, another cry for help. So back in the river again, reaching, pulling, applying, breathing and then another yell. Again and again, without end, goes the sequence. You know, I am so busy jumping in, pulling them to shore, applying artificial respiration, that I have no time to see who the hell is upstream pushing them all in. (Zola, cited in McKinlay, 1981, pp. 484-85)

This story illustrates the need to refocus "upstream," to think about solving the problem instead of only addressing short-term solutions, no matter how necessary such short-term work may be.

Studies that look no further than the victims of a social process remind us of the following old story. A man walking down a street one night passed an inebriated man crawling around on the sidewalk under a streetlight apparently looking for something on the ground. The first man asked the man on the ground, "What are you looking for?" The man on the ground replied, "My wallet." The first man then said, "It doesn't appear to be here. Are you sure you dropped it here?" To which the man on the ground replied, "No, I didn't drop it here. I dropped it back down the street where it's dark, but there's more light here."

It would appear that in seeking answers to the problems of disadvantaged African-Americans many scholars and policymakers tend to look where there is "more light," at the victims of social processes rather than the social processes that produce these victims. The orientation of this volume, as well as the series[1] of which it is a part, is one that sees African-Americans embedded in a network of mutually interdependent relationships with the local community and with the wider society. We study these individuals but consider them as groups of individuals acting and being acted upon by various societal institutions. An implicit question, then, is how does a particular societal institution help or hinder the progress of African-Americans?

In examining the societal context of economic trends we see that earnings and unemployment are a direct result of the changing structure of the labor market along with racial discrimination limiting entry to the remaining pools of jobs. Increasing poverty is seen as a result of rising female unemployment along with decreasing welfare benefits. The decline in the college-going rate of African-Americans is correlated with the change in scholarship support from grants to loans, which are more difficult for black than white Americans because of the smaller percentage of families who are able to take out such loans.

This volume addresses the interactions of African-Americans with the social, economic, political, and justice institutions of American life. Other volumes in this series address other areas of African-American life.

As the title of the first chapter, "Stratification and Subordination: Change and Continuity," by Moss and Reed suggests, in some instances the situations of African-Americans have changed and in some instances they have not. This chapter examines racial stratification, subordination, and change in various aspects of American life and concludes that despite improvements, racial stratification has not changed in any fundamental sense. The basic structural position of African-Americans has remained the same. The authors assert that legal doctrines and the courts have always provided justification and legality for whatever structural form the system of racial stratification has taken, and that several social factors—attitudes, values, ideology, and racial violence—operate to reinforce domination.

In the next chapter, "Race and Inequality in the Managerial Age," Darity, Cotton, and Hill discuss changes in the structure of the U.S. economy. They describe the changes as a shift from capitalism to managerialism, a phenomenon where more authority is given to experts in social analysis, policymaking, and management. Darity and his colleagues observe that persons with low levels of skill have few places in this economy and that the usual forms of job discrimination squeeze African-Americans out as there is less need for the occupations to which they previously had access. At the same time, we see that African-Americans are receiving less access to higher eduction. This development is significant since in this age of science and technology, colleges and universities assign credibility and credentials for the important positions in the economy Darity describes.

Darity et al. also examine the contradictions in the economics literature of the 1970s and 1980s. During the 1970s some economists painted rosy pictures of the economic progress of African-Americans. Yet in the 1980s other economists painted different pictures. Darity et al. demonstrate that the early optimistic views did not reflect the full reality of black male/white male income disparities.

In the chapter "Political Participation," Moss and her collaborators review trends in black voter registration and voting from 1940 to the present. They evaluate the impact and significance of black voting, address the role and function of political movements, and describe the political context within which the search for power continues to occur. Black political participation over the last 50 years has, they argue, included conventional and nonconventional politics, with much of the political participation before the passage of the Voting Rights Act of 1965 occurring in the form of protests and political movements. Moss and her collaborators conclude that despite a significant increase in the number of elected black officials in the United States during the past 25 years there is a continuing need for nonconventional politics because conventional politics are limited in affecting the status of African-Americans.

A critical indication of the status of a minority group in a society is its relationship with the institutions that administer justice. It is often these institutions that define and maintain the political status of minority group members, as the law is primarily an instrument of those who have power. In "Administration of Justice," Reed et al. explore the issue of African-

Americans and the administration of justice by examining sentencing, capital punishment, and juvenile courts. They also address the interaction of crime, drugs, and race. Referenced studies show that race is still a consistent factor in criminal sentencing. Juvenile courts, the authors argue, are critical institutions to consider in examining African-Americans and the criminal justice system because it is in these courts that many blacks with criminal careers get their first "record."

After years of studies demonstrating racial disparities in the application of the ultimate legal sanction—the death penalty—the U.S. Supreme Court in 1987 made such studies moot by ruling that discrepancies in the imposition of the death penalty do not violate the equal protection clause of the Fourteenth Amendment. Reed et al. describe the ruling in *McCleskey v. Kemp* (1987) as reminiscent of the *Plessy* (1896) ruling. The *McCleskey* ruling, they note, provides legal justification for the discriminatory application of the death penalty.

Although the bulk of the definitive research has been done on racial differences in sentencing and capital punishment, it is clear that race is a significant factor in earlier stages of the administration of justice as well. These stages involve the police and prosecutors. This chapter demonstrates that although the status of African-Americans in their relationship with the administration of justice has improved since the 1940s there is still a great distance to go to obtain equal justice.

NOTE

1. Other volumes in this series are *Education of African-Americans* (1991), *Research on the American Family: A Holistic Perspective* (1993), and *Health and Medical Care of African-Americans* (1993).

REFERENCES

Billingsley, A. (1986). *Black families in white America*. Englewood Cliffs, NJ: Prentice-Hall.

Brown v. Board of Education, 347 U.S. 483 (1954).

Jacobs, J. (1989). Black America, 1988: An overview. In J. Dewart (Ed.), *The state of black America 1989*, New York: National Urban League.

McCleskey v. Kemp, 481 U.S. 279 (1987).

McKinlay, J. B. (1981). A case for refocussing upstream: The political economy of illness. In P. Conrad and R. Kerns (Eds.), *The sociology of health and illness: Critical perspectives*, pp. 484–500. New York: St. Martin's Press.

Plessy v. Ferguson, 163 U.S. 537 (1896).

Simms, M. C. (1988). *Black economic progress: An Agenda for the 1990's.* Washington, DC: Joint Center for Political Studies.

AFRICAN-AMERICANS

1

Stratification and Subordination: Change and Continuity

E. Yvonne Moss and Wornie L. Reed, with Alphonso Pinkney, James Turner, and Sidney Wilhelm

One of the measures used to gauge progress made by African-Americans in gaining equal opportunity has been to compare and contrast the status of black Americans to that of white Americans using various social indices. Historically, the status of blacks relative to whites has been one of subordination; race has been a primary factor in determining social stratification and political status. Relations between white and black Americans were established during slavery and the Jim Crow era of segregation. In the infamous *Dred Scott* decision, U.S. Supreme Court Chief Justice Taney articulated the fundamental nature of this system of racial stratification: "Blacks have no rights which whites are bound to respect" (Bell, 1980a).

James Baldwin (1985) perceptively observed that in the sea change from the old worlds to the new, French, English, Spanish, and other Europeans "became white," while the Tokolor, Mandinka, Fulani, and other Africans "became black." Black and white became racial labels denoting power and status. Blacks were slaves; whites were free. Elimination of property requirements in the nineteenth century extended the franchise to all white men, and the passage of the Nineteenth Amendment (in the twentieth century) extended the franchise to white women. Not until the passage of the Voting Rights Act of 1965 was the franchise extended to all black Americans; and not until the *Brown* decision of 1954 were black Americans granted equal protection under the law. The Civil War outlawed slavery, but it did not eliminate stratification and privilege based on race. White domination continued through segregation laws and practices. The *Brown* decision, the civil rights movement, the Civil Rights Act of 1964, and the Voting Rights Act of 1965 ushered in a new era of race relations. After 300 years of slavery and 100 years of legalized racial oppression, the relations between white and black Americans were now to be based on "equality." The "age of equality," however, has not been accompanied by an end to white domination.

Scholars in this study have sought to evaluate developments in race relations, particularly since 1940, by examining racial stratification, subordination, and change in various areas of American life. Our general conclusion is that despite improvements in various aspects of American life, racial stratification has not changed in any fundamental sense. In addition to the structural mechanisms that perpetuate differential status, researchers point to social factors—attitudes, values, ideology, and racial violence—that reinforce racial domination. Legal doctrines and the courts have always provided justification and legality for whatever structural form the system of racial stratification has taken. Historically, the U.S. Constitution has been one of the primary supports for white supremacy.

FROM SLAVERY TO EQUALITY

Relations between black and white Americans are now established by the equality expectations based on the Constitution. This document, which originally sanctioned slavery, then segregation, has since 1954 given legal sanction to the principle of equality. At the time of the American Revolution slavery was sanctioned by the Constitution as a form of white property rights. The concepts of equality articulated by colonists in revolt blurred class distinctions between poor and rich whites, promoting affinity and solidarity at a time when these class distinctions could have undermined the war of liberation against the British.

After independence, an expansion of civil liberties for whites was accompanied by a contraction of civil rights for blacks. Slavery, recognized in the Constitution as a political and economic phenomenon rather than a moral one, provided the essential ingredient by which lower-class whites and upper-class whites could share a common identity as "free men." Slavery, and the racism that justified it, provided a way by which poor whites could feel simultaneously superior to enslaved blacks and equal to rich whites in spite of a distinctly different social and class status. In order to maintain this white American kinship, there was the need to keep black Americans in "their place." Citizenship, national identity, and social status in the emerging United States were increasingly defined in terms of race and color. Although Jacksonian Democracy removed property qualifications to extend the franchise for white males, in 1840 most free blacks were legally denied the right to vote.

From the beginning, the Constitution gave the wealthy "planter class" (approximately 7% of all slaveholders) disproportionate power, both nationally and locally. A majority of the justices on the Supreme Court between 1789 and 1865 were themselves slaveowners. Up until the Civil War, constitutional interpretation did not violate the economic and political imperatives of a slave economy dominated by a white, male, landed aristocracy.

After the war, the Civil War Amendments (Thirteenth, Fourteenth, and Fifteenth) along with Reconstruction provided a halting start toward a new basis of race relations. These nascent efforts were brought to an end, however, with the Hayes-Tilden Compromise in 1877 and the withdrawal of Union troops from the South. Racial discrimination against blacks increased at the same time that political democratization increased for whites. In a major test of the Fourteenth Amendment, the Supreme Court legitimized corporations but not the rights of black citizens in the 1873 *Slaughter-House Case(s)*. In those cases, the due process clause of the Fourteenth Amendment, which would become so vital to the restructuring of black-white relations in the mid-twentieth century, was interpreted to provide more protection for corporations (deemed legally to be "persons") than to African-Americans (Bell, 1980b).

The struggles of black Americans and their allies against segregation during the nineteenth and twentieth centuries culminated in the *Brown* decisions (1954 and 1955), the Civil Rights Act of 1964, and the Voting Rights Act of 1965. The White House's support for the modern civil rights movement of the sixties seemed to herald at long last the arrival of the equality revolution. For the first time since the existence of the Freedmen's Bureau during the Reconstruction period, governments not only made laws but constituted themselves as instruments of egalitarian policy. Above all, the courts were now obliged to examine constitutional principles in the light of egalitarian pressures.

With the emergence of the "age of equality," a number of important questions have been raised about race relations, law, and stratification. Can equality expectations eliminate racism and stratification by race and assure that there are no special advantages distributed according to race? Are there economic incentives and penalties capable of inducing the white elite to forsake segregation? And is it possible that equality will actually sustain, rather than relieve, white domination?

Examination of the issues raised by such questions has led some scholars to argue that although the application of equality is perceived as the extension of democratic principles to all—regardless of race, creed, color, or sex—it is more likely that the equality principle is serving white interests more than those of black people.

Historically, advances for African-Americans have been the result of policies primarily intended to serve white interests rather than to provide remedies for racial injustices (Bell, 1980b). Thus, scholars need to examine the contemporary "age of equality" for mechanisms that promote white self-interests at the expense of African-Americans.

For instance, one social analyst concludes that just as segregation "shifted" racism out of slavery to assure white exploitation of black labor, so equality "shifts" racism out of segregation to assure the economic demise rather than the exploitation of black people. Socioeconomic disparities coexist with the opportunity for equal rights under the Constitution. Supreme Court rulings have not outlawed racism, it is argued, but instead have actually endorsed a new form of racism to justify white oppression of black Americans. The notion of equality today, then, is as much a racist doctrine as were slavery and segregation (Wilhelm, 1987).

The established image of "equality" has meant that African-Americans can possess all manner of civil rights in the abstract, but little property. Wealth remains in white hands so that even under this so-called equality the social results are the same. The equality doctrine both masks and justifies the prevailing inequalities. Mechanisms other than color distinction are employed to subjugate black citizens. Growing disparities between black and white Americans coincide with the legal expansion of equal rights. The vigorous replacement of segregation by equality occurs at the same time that black people are being eliminated from the economy.

SOCIOECONOMIC STATUS

Economically, black America is in crisis. The average annual income of black families is 57% that of white families. The average net worth of black American families in 1986 was $3,397, compared to $39,135 for white families, a difference of almost 1,200%. In 1985 a National Urban League study indicated that with persistent unemployment and expanding poverty, African-Americans were being left out of the nation's economic recovery. If current trends continue to the year 2000, only 30% of all black men will be employed. Just as the abolition of slavery did not eradicate racism or the patterns of structural bias based on race, the equality doctrine has also failed to do so. Ironically, contemporary interpretations of the equality principle based on the Constitution seek a "color-blind" society that perpetuates inequality based on race.

When economics, employment, and social class are examined, the continued importance of race is clearly evident. While discrimination has lessened in jobs and training programs, racially exclusive practices remain. Limitations on mobility because of race affect the black elite as well as the black poor. The most strikingly favorable indication of racial change is the growth of the middle class among African-Americans. In 1982, using constant dollars, almost 25% of black families had incomes over $25,000 as compared to 8.7% in 1960 (Taylor, 1984).

This occupational mobility is a product of three factors: affirmative action, the expansion of public sector employment, and higher levels of education. Between 1966 and 1982 the number of black college students increased from 340,000 to over one million. A number of indicators, however, tend to suggest that such mobility may be slowed if not reversed in the near future. Between 1980 and 1984, black college enrollment dropped by 3%. Concomitantly, the more precarious economic status of black members of the middle class makes them more vulnerable than their white counterparts to economic downturns, government budget cuts, and changes in affirmative action policy.

The black middle class is proportionately smaller than the white middle class and is skewed more toward the lower than the upper part of the statistical group. Black professionals occupy lower paying jobs in lower prestige fields than white professionals. Black families tend to be more dependent on two or more wage-earners to maintain their middle-class status than are white families. Higher proportions of married women in black households work than married women in white households. These factors, along with a lower net worth and fewer resources, mean that black middle-class families are not as able as white middle-class families to transmit their class position to their children. In some cities—Atlanta, Philadelphia, New York, Los Angeles, Chicago, Oakland, and the District of Columbia, for example—the growth of middle-class economic status is still significant. However, there is less hope generally for economic advancement for other African-Americans trapped in poverty in urban and rural areas than there was in the sixties.

Noteworthy progress was made between 1959 and 1969 in reducing poverty among African-Americans. The percentage of black citizens who were poor dropped in that decade from 45% to 25%, and the official black family poverty rate declined from 48% to 28%. The net reduction in the number of poor black families was 494,000. However, during the 1970s this black economic progress was reversed as the percentage of blacks who were poor in 1979 had declined less than .5% during that decade, from 28% to 27.6%, and the black portion of the poor increased to 31%. Over

300,000 more black families were poor in 1979 than in 1969, thus canceling the gains made in the previous decade (Cross, 1984).

The dimensions of the socioeconomic crisis are even more evident from an examination of the consequences of these worsening economic conditions. More than one-half of all black children grow up in poverty. Unemployment among black teenagers has increased. Many young black men, unsuccessful in school and unable to find legitimate work, turn to hustling and crime. Homicide has become a leading cause of death among young black females as well as among young black males. The economic crisis among the poor has reduced the proportion of black men who work. Traditionally, blacks have been more likely than white men to be in the labor force. Since 1970, however, blacks have been less likely to be in the labor force (Swinton, 1990), and many black workers are unemployed or underemployed. Some analysts estimate that less than one-half of black men are engaged in steady work.

RESIDENTIAL SEGREGATION

In the area of housing, racial bias has remained pervasive. Throughout most of the half century that the federal government has been involved in housing and urban development, national policies have compounded and supported the discriminatory practices of realtors, banks, insurance companies, and lending companies. A review of major national policy initiatives by officials in the legislative, executive, and judicial branches of government indicates that during most of the past 50 years federal policies favored segregation and discrimination in housing.

Housing discrimination and the urbanization of blacks throughout the country have led to what some call the development of black "ghettos." Kenneth Clark (1965), for example, referring to this phenomenon, has written: "The dark ghetto's invisible walls have been created by the white society, by those who have power, both to confine those who have *no* power and to perpetuate their powerlessness." He continues, "The dark ghettos are social, political, educational, and—above all—economic colonies. Their inhabitants are subject peoples, victims of the greed, cruelty, insensitivity, guilt, and fear of their masters" (p. 11).

In the same vein, the U.S. National Advisory Commission on Civil Disorders, established after the widespread destruction accompanying rebellions in black communities throughout the United States, reported in 1968 that "what white Americans have never understood—but what the Negro can never forget—is that white society is deeply implicated in the ghetto. White institutions created it, white institutions maintain it, and white society condones it" (p. 2).

The federal government has been involved in housing and urban development for nearly half a century, and throughout most of that time the policies of the government favored segregation and discrimination against minorities in housing. It was not until 1962 that minimal steps were taken to curb these practices. This has led to the conclusion that "indeed, the net effect of Federal involvement in housing and urban development has been largely to perpetuate housing discrimination and patterns of housing segregation. In many cases, the Federal government has been a major force in exacerbating those problems" (U.S. Commission on Civil Rights, 1983, p. 133).

The following represent the major legislative, executive, and judicial actions supporting fair housing policies since 1940:

- 1948: In *Shelly v. Kraemer* (1948) the Supreme Court held that judicial enforcement of racially restrictive covenants violated the Fourteenth Amendment to the Constitution.
- 1962: President John Kennedy issued Executive Order 11063 on equal opportunity in housing. The order was designed to eliminate discrimination in federally assisted housing.
- 1964: Title VI of the Civil Rights Act was enacted, prohibiting discrimination in programs or activities receiving federal assistance by way of loan or grant.
- 1968: Congress passed the Civil Rights Act of 1968. This law established the "policy of the United States to provide, within Constitutional limitations, for fair housing throughout the United States." This act contains Title VIII, which prohibits discrimination in most of the nation's housing, both public and private. It also prohibits discrimination in mortgage lending and the advertising of housing. There have also been amendments to strengthen the law in the years since its first enactment.
- 1968: In *Jones v. Mayer* (1968) the Supreme Court upheld an 1866 civil rights law that bars "all racial discrimination, private and public, in the sale or rental of property."
- 1968: The Housing and Urban Development Act of 1968 was enacted establishing new programs of subsidized housing for lower income families.

Prior to 1962 there were three separate housing markets in the United States: one for blacks, one for whites, and one for mixed occupancy (U.S. Commission on Civil Rights, 1983, p. 3). The federal government accepted and even supported these discriminatory practices. Racial homogeneity was considered to be essential for stability in rental areas, and it was felt that any change in occupancy patterns would lead to a decline in property values. At the same time blacks were excluded from the suburbs. The Executive Order of the President in 1962 did little, if anything, to foster fair housing policies.

The 1964 Civil Rights Act likewise had little or no effect on open housing. However, four years later the Civil Rights Act of 1968 established for the first time a comprehensive fair housing program, making it illegal to discriminate in almost all housing, public and private. What was lacking, however, was vigorous enforcement of the provisions of this act.

Little has been accomplished toward the goal of fair housing, and since the beginning of the Reagan administration in 1981 the federal government has moved away from vigorously enforcing fair housing laws, maintaining that voluntary compliance is the principal mechanism for fair housing (U.S. Commission on Civil Rights, 1983, pp. 140–41). This hardly serves the cause of fair housing, for voluntary compliance means no compliance. Among the first acts of this administration was the withdrawal of the interpretive regulations of the Civil Rights Act of 1968. The Department of Justice has curtailed its enforcement efforts to the point where it has virtually abandoned the area of fair housing. And the government has reduced, and in some cases eliminated, efforts to eliminate the data required to determine whether violations of the Civil Rights Act of 1968 have taken place. In short, one is forced to agree with the following assessment:

> The federal government currently exhibits no enthusiasm in carrying out its statutory and constitutional mandates of nondiscrimination in housing. Indeed, the government, measured by its action during the present administration, appears to be engaged in an effort to dismantle the very legal and programmatic structure by which the fragile foundation of fair housing has been painfully built over the past three decades. (U.S. Commission on Civil Rights, 1983, p. 134)

Discrimination in housing today remains pervasive, as several studies indicate (Danielson, 1976; Feagin & Feagin, 1986; National Committee Against Discrimination in Housing, n.d.; Struyk, 1976; U.S. Commission on Civil Rights, 1974, 1975; U.S. Department of Housing and Urban Development, 1984). Discrimination is widespread in the rental and sale of housing, in urban and suburban regions, and in public and private housing. Although the federal government finally has a stated policy of fair housing for all Americans, it has been far from diligent in curbing housing discrimination. The Department of Housing and Urban Development and the Department of Justice are responsible for compliance with fair housing laws, but neither agency has effectively enforced the laws.

The Housing Market Practices Survey (U.S. Department of Housing and Urban Development, 1979), for example, conducted one of the largest studies of its type in 1977 and concluded that

- Discrimination in the housing market persists on a significant scale in all areas of the United States.
- The practices are frequently subtle and require sophisticated techniques for detection.
- Massive skillful enforcement efforts will be required to eradicate these practices.

The residential segregation of blacks actually increased in the 1940s, 1950s, and 1960s. Between 1950 and 1970 black neighborhoods in 20 large cities, where they represented three-fourths of the population, increased from 30% to 51% while the proportion of blacks in mixed neighborhoods with 25% or fewer blacks declined from 25% to 16% (Levitan et al., 1973, p. 227).

One of the few empirical measures of discrimination in housing is the segregation index. Developed by Karl E. Taeuber and Alma F. Taeuber (1972), the index can be used to measure increases in housing segregation over time and to compare cities and regions of the country. It assumes values between 0 to 100. The higher the index, the greater the degree of racial segregation; conversely, the lower the index, the less the degree of racial segregation in housing. For example, the Taeubers report that Indianapolis, Indiana, had a segregation index of 90.4 in 1940, 91.4 in 1950, and 91.6 in 1960. This means that in Indianapolis the extent of segregation in housing increased steadily for three decades (p. 40).

As the Taeubers report, "In a city where Negroes constitute half of the population, the residents of any city block would be about equally divided between Negroes and whites. In a city where Negroes constitute 10 percent of the population, one of every ten households in each block might be expected to be Negro" (p. 29). The index has been computed for several decades, although the number of cities included in each period varies.

Taeuber and Taeuber's national housing segregation index indicates that America's cities are only slightly less segregated today than they were in 1940. The index in 1940 was 85.2. By 1950 that figure had worsened to 87.3. In 1960 there was a slight drop to 86.1, but the segregation index increased during that decade to 87.0. The decade from 1970 to 1980 showed a drop from 87.0 to 81.0. Clearly, America's neighborhoods continue to be "homogeneous" (racially segregated) despite new laws and public proclamations (Reed, 1989).

As these data indicate, discrimination in housing is widespread, and there appears to be little promise for substantially reducing it in the near future. One writer has suggested that with the 6-point drop in the average segregation index for urban areas in the 1970s, "It will take another half century to half desegregate these cities. Some cities, such as Chicago, St. Louis, and Washington, will take centuries to be fully desegregated" (U.S. Commission on Civil Rights, 1983, p. 144).

Extensive suburbanization occurred in the United States after World War II, but suburban housing was intended for whites, not blacks. Although it is estimated that the number of blacks living in the suburbs increased by 28.3%, from 758,000 to 3,433,000, between 1960 and 1970, such growth was not uniform throughout the country (U.S. Commission on Civil Rights, 1983, p. 31). For example, it is estimated that one-sixth of the increase was in the suburbs of Washington, DC. In addition, seven standard metropolitan statistical areas contained about 55% of black suburbanites in 1980 (U.S. Commission on Civil Rights, 1983, p. 31).

From 1950 through 1970, blacks accounted for slightly more than 5% of suburban residents (Dolce, 1976, p. 82). During the 1970s the metropolitan areas with the largest volumes of black suburban growth experienced low or declining rates of growth. Data indicate that the black population of the suburbs rose from 2.5 million in 1960 to 3.6 million in 1970, and nearly 6.2 million in 1980 (U.S. Commission on Civil Rights, 1983, p. 4). The number of black suburbanites increased because "in a number of cities, ghettos have expanded beyond the city line and into the inner suburbs" (Orfield, 1981, p. 54).

Most suburban blacks live in the rings surrounding the largest cities in the country. It is estimated that the proportion of blacks in these areas was about 3% for decades (Farley, 1970, p. 514). In the 1960s the black population in the suburban rings increased slightly. In addition to the suburban rings, older, more densely populated suburbs witnessed a growth in black population, as did some of the new suburban developments.

The U.S. Commission on Civil Rights reported in 1975 that while suburban blacks are more integrated with whites than those in central cities, most suburban blacks live in places that "resemble their sister central cities rather than new growth, suburban areas and hence do not fit the common concept of suburbs" (p. 131). By 1970, only one suburban resident in 20 was black, "and even then was likely to reside in a disproportionately black suburb next to a central city ghetto. . . . This overwhelming degree of segregation seems unlikely to have occurred merely by chance" (Feagin & Feagin, 1986, p. 86).

One must conclude that fair housing practices are virtually nonexistent in America's suburbs. Although some blacks have moved to the suburbs, especially since 1960, this in no way indicates a change in residential patterns for African-Americans. They continue to be concentrated in central cities throughout the country, and where they have moved to the suburbs, it has been in those areas adjacent to large cities. Hence, the "residential segregation patterns of central cities are reappearing in the suburbs" (Farley, 1970, p. 517).

The slow desegregation of white suburbs and neighborhoods is only one aspect of the housing crisis. Progress toward access to safe, affordable, adequate housing has been nil. Public housing projects have generally been failures; often these projects have further isolated poor black people from the rest of society. Inadequate delivery of public services and the absence of competitive and diverse private retail and financial services contribute to the general crisis in housing as well as to other aspects of social and economic deprivation.

WHITE ATTITUDES

Economic deprivation and social deprivation have been the consequences of racial stratification. The system of domination that institutionalizes race-based access to opportunity structures is both reflected in and reinforced by attitudes of white and black Americans. It is interesting to note that the longest running topic in survey research has been the evaluation of white attitudes toward African-Americans. Since World War II, issues related to race in survey research have changed in two ways: the kinds of issues addressed and the ascriptive characteristics associated with the attributes "progressive" and "regressive." Changes in law have made many issues moot. Surveys of white attitudes today indicate that regional differences are less distinct. White attitudes toward black Americans have become more uniform throughout the country.

White Americans still exhibit the duality of orientation that Ellison (1964) labeled "ethical schizophrenia" in the 1940s. By this he meant that white Americans demonstrated a sincere belief in the values of democracy, while condoning and justifying decidedly undemocratic treatment of black citizens. Today scholars use the term "symbolic racism" to explain how white Americans can hold egalitarian general racial attitudes at the same time as they disapprove or oppose policies that seek to operationalize equality (cf. Schuman, Steeh, & Bobo, 1985; Bobo, 1983; Kinder & Sears, 1991; McConahay & Hough, 1976).

There have been increases in both interracial attitudes about social contact and (to a lesser extent) increases in black penetration of white neighborhoods and churches. But the data suggest that the increases in the social and spatial *proximity* of blacks and whites do not necessarily result in increased social *interaction* (Smith, 1988).

At face value, whites seem to adhere to the principles of racial equality and interaction. But whenever the contexts of such interactions are specified, opposition is raised. A look at post–World War II changes in attitudes toward varying degrees of school desegregation may shed some light on this issue. As shown in Table 1.1, between 1958 and 1986 almost all whites came to accept the presence of a few blacks in school with their children. But note that if the question is posed such that half of the children in the desegregated school are black, tolerance drops an average of approximately 20%. When the question is asked about majority black schools, as many as half of those tolerant of half-black schools become intolerant. Further, while there are increases in tolerance of a few blacks and half-black schools over time, there is relatively little improvement in white attitudes toward majority black schools.

In schools with a few blacks, the likelihood of any one white child interacting with a black child is extremely low. But all other things being equal, in half-black schools this likelihood of interracial interaction theoretically increases to around 50%, and in majority black schools it should exceed 50%. So as long as the *intensity* of the interracial experience is quite low, whites seem more willing to participate. But as this intensity increases, the attractiveness of the situation decreases. The racial attitudes of whites are directly proportional to the amount of interaction structured by the potential interracial context. Note that the desegregation of public accommodations, transportation, and so on, can be accepted because the amount of interaction it *compels* for participants is low, while the relatively intense social contact of interracial dining is avoided.

This group position approach was first postulated by Blumer (1958) and empirically validated in time-series analyses of attitudes toward both interracial housing (Smith, 1982) and school desegregation (Smith, 1981). While the largest component of racial attitude change involves simultaneous change across all subgroups of whites, a substantial component of the incremental *increase in tolerance* over time stems from cohort replacement, that is, younger persons replacing older persons in the surveys. Further, *decreases in tolerance* among whites accrue as a result of increased educational attainment over time (Smith, 1985).

Table 1.1
Attitudes of Whites Toward Varying Degrees of School Desegregation, 1958–1986[a]

Survey Year	Percent in Favor of Attending Schools With A Few Black Students	50% Black Students	>50% Black Students
1958[b]	74.2	48.5	31.6
1959	79.6	52.8	29.7
1963	77.8	48.4	26.7
1965[c]	83.2	57.9	31.7
1966	87.5	57.3	32.4
1969	88.4	61.8	34.6
1970[c]	91.0	68.4	35.4
1972	94.0	74.7	44.8
1973	91.8	64.4	91.0
1974	95.7	66.9	33.4
1975[c]	94.1	68.1	36.0
1977	92.8	73.5	35.8
1978[c]	93.8	69.0	36.3
1980	94.2	71.6	38.4
1982	95.8	79.4	45.5
1983	96.5	74.9	35.1
1985	95.7	77.6	40.2
1986	96.2	76.4	36.3

[a]Over 96.2% of all nonblack respondents are white. Includes only those respondents living in a home with school-aged children.

[b]All surveys conducted by the American Institute of Public Opinion (Gallup) or the National Opinion Research Center (NORC). All sampling errors ≤ 5%.

[c]These issues appeared in two Gallup surveys in both 1965 and 1970 and in one Gallup and one NORC survey in both 1975 and 1978. The percentages given are the mean results from both surveys in those years.

Source: Racial Insularity at the Core: Contemporary American Racial Attitudes, by A. Wade Smith, 1988, *Trotter Review, 2*(2) p. 11, Boston, MA: University of Massachusetts, William Monroe Trotter Institute.

This data and the results of other surveys suggest that not much racial attitude change should be expected in the near future. All of the big (and easy) changes have been incorporated into public policy. Partially as a result, there is little interest in white attitudes regarding these moot issues. With the possible exception of school desegregation, those areas of racial contact remaining are beyond the regulation of law. In short, the amount of interracial personal contact any white experiences is the result of a series of extremely personal decisions, and it seems as though most will not extend themselves very much in that direction.

It appears that just as whites do not seem to be extending themselves toward blacks, they also do not want blacks to intrude into their lives. Both Gallup and NORC have surveyed whites on their attitudes regarding the intrusion of blacks into "their world." Over time, these four specific questions were repeated most frequently:

Which statement comes closest to how you, yourself, feel: Blacks shouldn't push themselves where they are not wanted. (Agree strongly, agree slightly, disagree slightly, disagree strongly)

White people have a right to keep blacks out of their neighborhoods if they want to, and blacks should respect that right. (Agree strongly, agree slightly, disagree slightly, disagree strongly)

Suppose there is a community-wide vote on the general housing issue. There are two possible laws to vote on (respondent reads an open and a restricted housing law). Which law would you vote for?

In general, do you favor or oppose busing of black and white school children from one district to another?

According to Table 1.2, only a little more than a third of all whites would accept the legitimacy of blacks pushing for desegregation in the face of white resistance. In other words, even in the 1980s, a sentiment of racial insularity exists among an overwhelming majority of nonblacks. Note that there has been only a slight erosion in these feelings since the 1960s. It seems that while a majority of the white population willingly coexists with blacks in desegregated work, school, and other public settings, in reality they want as little to do with blacks as possible.

This sentiment becomes glaringly apparent when specific public policies surrounding interracial contact are at issue. While the overwhelming majority would limit such actions, more than a quarter of all whites would give some respect to the "right" of whites to bar blacks from their neighborhoods (see Table 1.2), and these respondents would call for blacks to yield a similar respect. In other words, a substantial plurality of whites

Table 1.2
Public Policy–Oriented Racial Attitudes, 1963–1986[a]

Survey Year	Percent of White Respondents[b]			
	Disagree That Blacks Should Intrude	Disagree w/Black "Rights" to a Segregated Neighborhood	Would Vote for Open Housing Law	Favor Busing
1963	22.3	44.9	---	---
1966	21.9	---	---	---
1968	20.6	43.2	---	---
1970	15.6	50.6	---	13.5
1971	---[c]	---	---	17.8[d]
1972	31.9[d]	59.2[d]	---	19.5
1973	26.0	---	---	34.1
1974	---	---	---	20.1
1975	24.8	---	34.0	17.2
1976	28.5	59.6	34.6	15.8
1977	26.5	55.9	---	16.3
1978	---	---	36.8	20.2
1980	31.1	64.8	38.8	---
1982	39.3	70.2	---	19.2
1983	---	---	44.4	23.1
1984	39.9	71.7	48.7	---
1985	38.2	72.3	---	22.0
1986	---	---	47.1	29.4

[a]All surveys conducted by the American Institute of Public Opinion (Gallup) or the National Opinion Research Center (NORC). All sampling errors $\leq$ 5%. See text for actual question wordings.
[b]Over 96.2% of all nonblack respondents are white.
[c]The dashed line indicates that this issue did not appear in any survey during this particular year.
[d]This is the mean response from two or more surveys that asked this question in this year.
Source: Racial Insularity at the Core: Contemporary American Racial Attitudes, by A. Wade Smith, 1988, *Trotter Review*, 2 (2) p. 11, Boston, MA: University of Massachusetts, William Monroe Trotter Institute.

see nothing wrong in restrictive covenants and other limitations to free-market real estate activities that are designed specifically to preserve the racial integrity of a community.

Table 1.2 also shows that less than a majority of whites would vote for an open housing law that "says that a homeowner cannot refuse to sell to someone because of his or her color." Presumably the majority would vote for the version wherein "a homeowner can decide for himself." Apparently it matters little to the quarter of the white population that would restrict blacks from living in their neighborhood or the majority of respondents who would circumvent such restrictive covenants via a series of individual decisions that the courts have long ruled such measures to be both illegal and actionable (i.e., the offended blacks can litigate to recover damages—including pain and suffering).

Not much change in racial attitudes is expected among white citizens in the near future because whites do not indicate a willingness to choose interracial contact. Contemporary surveys of whites indicate a reluctance to live with black neighbors, a desire to insulate themselves from contact with black people, and a desire to maintain a social distance from black Americans even while agreeing to formal legal and civil rights for black citizens. This suggests an insularity at the core of Euro-Americans' racial attitudes that may persist for some time. Such conclusions imply an even greater imperative for legal interpretation and government enforcement to promote equal justice and to move toward the breaking up of systems of white domination.

VALUE ORIENTATIONS OF BLACKS

Stratification by race in America has also influenced the development of values among African-Americans (Himes, 1974). Here, care should be taken—heeding the admonitions of Ellison—not to equate all value orientations among black people as reactions to white domination. The complex relations between the dominant white American culture and the black American subculture create a variety of sources for the development of social values among African-Americans. Scholars categorize these sources under two typologies: the traditional American value heritage and ideological orientations within black communities. While more work needs to be done on regional variations, rural orientations, and relationships between the two major types, four categories of value orientations have been identified within urban black communities: (1) socially integrated, (2) structurally integrated, (3) structurally isolated, and (4) the excluded sector (Himes, 1987).

Black people who evidence socially integrated values generally maintain contact with black churches, social clubs, and voluntary associations, even though these are primarily oriented toward the values of the white communities where they live. They wish to be "Americans" in the general sense, although the degree to which this means that they wish to be assimilated as "white" Americans is not clear. Individuals of this orientation are success-oriented, and they demonstrate little support or empathy for confrontational racial protests. Members of these black families develop racially self-directed and self-maintaining values at the same time as they develop civil rights and public-policy values for use in the larger, white, bureaucratic, formal world. Black families in this category who live and work in desegregated areas tend to equip themselves to live in two different social worlds.

Members of the structurally integrated category work and sometimes live in integrated settings. Most, however, live—and all of them socialize—in a segregated world. Those who live in black neighborhoods do so because they want it that way. They evidence a split value system. On the one hand, they live and work by general "white" American values. At the same time, they articulate well-known black values: that "black is beautiful"; that black history is an important part of their heritage; that Black English is acceptable; and that black people are as intelligent and capable as white people. Additionally, they exhibit vigorous civil rights and public-policy values.

Black people in the structurally isolated category are generally employed in low-skilled and service sectors of the economy. The class system in the United States isolates these citizens. The economic and work values of those who are structurally isolated are developed through jobs where workers tend to feel cheated and oppressed by those in control. Therefore, the orientation of these black people is not toward traditional values but toward communal and ideological values of black communities, although some of the traditional values of the group coincide with those of the dominant American values (i.e., values of Southern black culture and black church culture). Blacks in this category tend to advocate the self-regarding and self-maintenance values of popular black culture. They acknowledge the importance of black history, culture, and society. Black English is legitimized, and black heroes and heroines are idolized. These values sustain the sense of self-worth, boost morales, and serve to legitimize the cause of black people in the white-dominated society. Other value orientations among this group emphasize liberation, creative expression, and achievement. They support civil rights legislation and enforcement as well as the expansion of those gains already made. Collective action and confrontation are viewed as legitimate ways to pursue the struggle for black rights.

Members of the excluded sector are at the bottom of society in terms of economic and social indices. They are marginally employed or unemployed. They have little education and few marketable skills. Black people in this category are ill-housed, excluded from participation in the larger community, and alienated from the general society. Communications are generally broken with family, church, schools, media, and service agencies. Street life, the primary source of the development of values, does not function well to communicate and transmit traditional American values. In any case, many traditional values and social rules are ineffective in the real worlds that these people inhabit. Families in this grouping who stay in tune with traditional values are the exceptions.

Where do values come from in this grouping? They are improvised, borrowed, and developed pragmatically. Traditional values come to be viewed in pejorative and threatening terms. Indigenous values and norms are legitimized and enforced. There is evidence of hostility toward those in white communities as well as suspicion and distrust of white authority, especially the police. Members of this category exhibit support for civil rights efforts.

Elijah Anderson's work (1978) on marginally employed or unemployed black men in Chicago suggests a slightly different interpretation. According to Anderson, there are special hangouts in the cities that serve as gathering places for the urban poor and working-class people who seek a sense of self-worth and status through their sociability and interaction with peers. Urban taverns and bars, barbershops, carryouts, and their adjacent street corners and alleys are examples of the places that serve similar functions for the poor as more formal social clubs or domestic circles do for the middle and upper classes.

Those who frequent these places create their own local, informal, social stratification system. Status within this system is action-oriented and precarious, based in large measure upon what people think and say and do about other members of the group. Extended primary groups develop in these places. Among the groups studied by Anderson the primary values were a "visible means of support" and "decency" (1978, p. 209). Residual values or values group members adopt after the "props" supporting decency have been judged to be unattainable or unavailable are "toughness," "gettin' big money," "gettin' some wine," and "having some fun."

Some writers have attempted to explain "low-class" values as weak imitations or approximations of the wider society's values. Rodman (1963), for example, has suggested that low-income people are unable to meet the larger society's standards of social conduct and therefore must stretch their own values to adjust to their particular life circumstances. Although there may be a certain amount of truth to this view, and it is supported by my own analysis, I believe it does not go far enough in appreciating the lives of the people involved and the internal coherence and integrity of their local stratification systems. The people I studied . . . appear not so much to "stretch" a given set of values to meet some general standard as to *create their own particular standards of social conduct* [emphasis added] along variant lines open to them. (Anderson, 1978, p. 210)

While this brief attempt to categorize black value orientations does not cover the entire spectrum of attitudes and values to be found among African-Americans, what is clear is that racial domination and the subordinate position of black Americans in society do influence the values espoused by black people as well as white people. The duality of values held is reminiscent of the concept of "twoness" employed by W.E.B. Du Bois in his 1903 book, *The Souls of Black Folk.* Interestingly, the reality of black peoples' lives, even for those who are classified as socially integrated, is one in which individuals and families exist in two different worlds, two different cultures, between which they must negotiate their existence.

SCIENTIFIC RACISM

There are in the dominant culture a number of mechanisms that reinforce and support white domination. These include ideologies of white supremacy. The most blatant contemporary ideological rationale for white domination is scientific racism.[1] Scientific racism is rooted in the idea that domination is a right of the biologically superior. Scientific racism has produced "evidence" sustaining the belief that black people are inherently inferior, thus rationalizing white rule.

The proponents of scientific racism advance arguments like those advocated by Social Darwinists earlier in this century. They argue for an educational system that will train the intellectually inferior for specific positions in the labor force. Also, again like the Social Darwinists, advocates of scientific racism view intelligence and achievement as products of innate genetic or cultural endowment. The logic of this has significant and potentially dangerous implications for social policy. If intelligence, achievement, mobility, and success are products of inherent biological or cultural differences that cannot be altered by environment, then it is folly to try to alter social structures or institutional practices to promote equality or equal opportunity. Scientific racism goes further than Social Darwinism in not only blaming the victim but also in providing a quantitative and quasi-scientific basis for perpetuating inequality and domination.

Traits presumed to be biologically determined become the basis for social policy. This substantially limits the opportunities for targeted groups and makes them the victims of exclusion, sometimes even of extermination. In this century, Nazi Germany is associated with the most developed and horrifying application of social policy based on ideas of scientific racism. Here in the United States, prominent writers and scholars have contributed to the development of this phenomenon, especially during the 1920s and 1930s. From the turn of the century through the 1930s scientific racism gained popularity in the United States in scholarly and popular literature. The enactment of the 1924 restrictive immigration bill may have been the highwater mark of the influence of these ideas during that period.

From the 1930s until the 1960s scientific racism was dormant. Now, however, the arguments have been resurrected in new forms. Gone are the archaic notions of phrenology and craniology that assumed that human worth and behavior could be determined by body type. Contemporary theorists seek instead to prove the primacy of heredity over environment in the determination of intelligence. The language is new, but the message is the same: Genetic endowment is the great divider between superior and inferior types. Such differences cannot be mediated through legislation or social policy. Hence, racial differences are an immutable fact that are ordained genetically.

Scientific racism has functioned as an influence on public action. Such perceptions of human differences are a convenient *raison d'être* for a stratified society. Some of the earliest theorists of the ideology of scientific racism were social scientists (Hofstadter, 1959; Schwendinger & Schwendinger, 1974). Preoccupied with social order and progress, they framed questions of individual and social difference as political questions. Their ideas, like all pseudoscientific ideas regarding the human species, found acceptance among those seeking to justify the subordination of others. In periods of major social change such ideas tend to intensify as status positions are challenged. The 1960s was such a period.

The *Brown* decision (1954) altered the legal status of African-Americans and proved to be a catalyst for the modern civil rights movement. The court's ruling also struck at the core of the ideology of scientific racism. The philosophy of separate but equal had existed under the assumption of biological differences. Thus the ideology of scientific racism had given support to those who sought to maintain entitlement and privilege.

Scientific racism sees entitlement as a just reward to those who are genetically superior. Conversely, genetic inferiority is seen as the basis for restricting entitlement and privilege. Because of the presumptions about the association between race and superiority and inferiority, race becomes the key variable in restricting or granting entitlement. Members of the white race, designated by the ideology as biologically superior, are thus entitled to a superordinate status and the social, economic, and political privileges that are accorded this status. Members of the black race, designated by the ideology as biologically inferior, are denied any entitlement and privileges and are relegated to a subordinate status.

The *Brown* decision was a critical turning point not only in education but in the larger society because it set the stage for major alterations in the system of entitlement. The court's decision not only called into question the denial of choice in education, but also suggested a tolerance for a realignment in the historic patterns of power. The sociopolitical movements of the 1950s and 1960s vigorously sought such a realignment in the patterns of power relations, challenging the entitlements and privileges historically bestowed on white Americans.

The reemergence of the ideology of scientific racism during the past two decades has taken the form of an attack on the mental capacity of black children—and, by implication, all black people—by means of a dubious and abusive interpretation of intelligence testing. Arthur Jensen at the University of California at Berkeley, William Shockley of Stanford, and Richard Herrnstein of Harvard were in the forefront of a debate over the education of black children, the use of intervention strategies, and the development of public policy options to limit population growth among "genetically inferior blacks." All of these concepts were based on presumptions that intelligence was 80% inherited and 20% environment. Thus, policies that tried to use public funds or initiatives to improve the education and performance of black children were deemed to be undemocratic because they granted the disadvantaged some unearned privilege.

The proponents of scientific racism ignored evidence of historical, social, and structural influences on intelligence testing and ignored the decline in SAT scores among white students as well. The emphasis on quantitative data, performed in an advocacy manner, was an attempt to give the resurfaced ideology of white supremacy an aura of scientific objectivity and respectability. The appeal to the inheritability of intelligence restates the same argument that social classes are products of differential genetic stock. Scientific racism is an attempt to make inferiority a matter of science rather than prejudice.

W.E.B. Du Bois (1940/1968) identified science and empire as the preeminent values in Western societies at the turn of the century. It should come as little surprise, then, that science during this century has been enlisted to justify political domination. The ideology of scientific racism has been invoked, in its least harmful form, as a rationalization for the insulation of privilege, the restraint of mobility, and the limitation of entitlement. In its most virulent form, scientific racism is a prescription for genocide.

The history of scientific racism is indicative of how data that purport to be "objective" may be used to promote reprehensible policy. Scientific racism has justified the deaths of countless millions of people by validating the claim that they were inferior and undeserving. A version of this ideology is being used today to justify the continuation of white domination and privilege.

RACIAL ANTAGONISM AND VIOLENCE

In a racially stratified society, racial violence is used as a method of social control to maintain the structures of subordination. In a conspicuously violent society so stratified, violence is used for political purposes to maintain a racially bifurcated system, controlled politically by whites.

Historically, patterns of racial violence in the United States have moved in cycles of latent and aggressive activity. Latent periods have been relatively benign. During these periods the superordinate-subordinate system of race relations has been characterized by a kind of white paternalism. Aggressive periods have ensued when the system of domination has been challenged and/or the benefits of white superordination have been perceived to be eroding. During these periods, aggression and violence have been used to terrorize black people; the foundations of racial progress built by blacks have become targets for attack. The ebb and flow of racial violence has followed shifts in the national political economy and changing patterns in the labor force and the labor markets.

All institutions in American society have been permeated by the stratified and segmented nature of race relations. Racially motivated violence is a legacy of these unequal race relations, and it is endemic to the national political culture. Although manifest throughout American history, racial violence has differed in form and significance, breadth, and intensity from period to period.

This racially segmented social structure, established and maintained by violence, generates both systematic oppression of nonwhite racial groups, especially African-Americans, and systematic privileges for whites. The system of white privilege provides the philosophical and material basis for racism among whites. These privileges are the "white rights" that those who perpetuate racial violence are dedicated to defending.

White supremacy and racial oppression have been major factors in the political and economic development of this nation. The function of racial violence has been to establish and to perpetuate this system of differential privilege and deprivation based on race. Racial violence is a deliberate activity that reinforces ideologies of racial supremacy and intimidates the victims of violence and racial oppression.

Racial violence is currently on the upturn, a reaction to at least two important social dynamics: (1) the dramatic changes brought about by progress in civil rights; and (2) the dramatic transformations in the infrastructure of national economic life that have generated (since the Great Depression) unprecedented levels of unemployment, poverty, homelessness, and social dislocation. Currently, large segments of the American population are experiencing a heightened sense of insecurity and vulnerability.

Historically, racism has had the force of legal sanction. The legal system was key to the structuring of the system of white supremacy and racial oppression in the country. The slave codes, black codes, immigration laws, Indian treaties, and Jim Crow system explicitly constructed a "color line" and made racism the undisputed law of the land. Such laws, with the support of the Supreme Court in landmark decisions like *Dred Scott* (1857) and *Plessy v. Ferguson* (1896) and a host of other lesser known but important rulings in federal appellate, state, and county courts, detailed the structure of the racist status quo in practically all fields of social life from the labor market to housing, from schools to churches, from politics to social organizations.

The present rise of racist violence can best be understood in the context of the broad antiracist social movements in the 1960s and the early 1970s. Agencies of the government, as well as nongovernmental organizations, resorted to violence as a general tactic of intimidation in an endeavor to resist, slow down, and ultimately destabilize the movement's political assault on racism wholesale in society. This period was the occasion for large-scale, frequent, racially motivated violence as the racists conducted open warfare against the black community. Hundreds of churches were bombed, thousands of people assaulted and banned from employment, dozens of civil rights workers wounded and murdered, including the assassinations of Jimmy Young, Mack Parker, Medgar Evers, Viola Liuzzo, Bobby Hutton, Fred Hampton, Malcolm X, and Martin Luther King, Jr., to name but a few.

The racial violence of the 1960s was an extension of the common practice of lynching, which was still fairly active throughout the 1940s and during the 1950s, even after it had been formally outlawed. The two decades of the post–World War II era were characterized by racially organized terror against the black community, particularly in the South. This reign of terror was responsible, in part, for the migration of hundreds of thousands of people out of the South. But in the face of this adversity, the civil rights struggles produced a mass antiracism resistance movement for democratic rights. As a popular coalition it was able to obtain legal victories that virtually destroyed the legal, if not political, basis of racism.

By the early 1970s, the black political movement had successfully compelled the government to adopt affirmative action and desegregation policies that dictated positive action against racial dualism. However, it was precisely this antiracist political and ideological momentum that some conservative movements, including the "new right" as well as the white nationalists, began to organize to reverse. Racist violence is a part of this counterattack. As in the past, racist violence is central to the effort to politically intimidate "minority" persons.

During the past decade several research centers have collected information on racially motivated violence.[2] A study of the data reveals an upsurge of racism and racist violence, with the most deadly attacks coming against the African-American community. There has been an increase in the number of incidents of white mobs attacking blacks in segregated residential areas. There has also been a steady increase in the firebombing of homes purchased by black families in predominantly white neighborhoods. A study of violence in residential neighborhoods conducted by the Southern Poverty Law Center indicates that between 1985 and 1986 there were at least 45 cases of vigilante activity directed at black families who were moving into predominantly white communities. In the last five years incidents of racial harassment or violence have been reported on over 300 college campuses (Wilkerson, 1990).

The events in Howard Beach that led to the death of Michael Griffith in 1986 and the killing of Yusef Hawkins in Bensonhurst in 1989 reflect a long-standing problem of racist violence in white communities in New York City. Racially motivated assaults had increased to at least one a week in 1987. The Chicago Police Department reported a 58% increase in racial attacks for the first six months of 1986 over the same period in 1985. The New York City Police Department reported an increase in racially motivated violence over the last eight years. These attacks go mostly unreported in the news media (Walters, 1987).

The Community Relations Service of the Justice Department and the Center for Democratic Renewal ("Hate and Violence," 1987) provide data that demonstrate a sharp upturn nationally in violent racial attacks. The increase was 42% between 1985 and 1986, fueled largely by the boldness of white terrorist groups in the United States. Nationally, the Community Relations Service of the Justice Department reports an increase in all cases of racial confrontations, from 953 in 1977 to 1,996 in 1982. The Justice Department also reported a 460% increase in cases of racial violence involving the Ku Klux Klan between 1978 and 1979, and a startling 550% increase in the period 1978 to 1980 (Walters, 1987).

The Ku Klux Klan has reemerged with vigor. The Klan has always functioned as the armed militia for white supremacy. In his study of the civil rights movement in the south, Bloom gives a penetrating view of the Klan (1987):

> The Ku Klux Klan was an instrument of the struggle. All classes in the white South appear to have been involved in it and to have used it for different purposes. In the predominantly white counties, which were usually located in the hills away from the fertile plantation areas, the Klan was used to drive Blacks out so as to eliminate them as competitors with white laborers . . . the upper class used the Klan to control Black labor, even to the detriment of white labor. Blacks who tried to leave the area were threatened with murder, and some of them were killed. When they did leave, they were sometimes dragged back, even across state lines. (p. 4)

What was most important in winning upper-class support for the Klan was its political character. It is clear that the Klan did not emerge because of confusion in the South. It was founded for a very conscious and specific purpose: to defend slavery and racism and to defeat Reconstruction and civil rights. The Klan has never disappeared; and the Klan is a major factor in the rising racist violence of the present period. There were more Klan rallies in the period 1978–1980 than in the rest of the 1970s.The Klan burst on the national scene again in 1979 with a planned rifle attack on participants at an anti-Klan rally in the heart of the city of Greensboro, North Carolina, in broad daylight and in full view of local television cameras and reporters. In the 1980s its activities spread to Illinois, Ohio, New Jersey, Pennsylvania, as far north as Vermont, Maine, and other northeast areas, and west to Colorado and California. Of course, the Klan is much smaller than it was years ago; and its strategies have also changed. The modern Klan seeks to shed the image of the night-rider vigilante for the role of street-level community organizer, where it motivates and directs alienation and anger in lower- and working-class white communities.

The question that begs consideration in an analysis of the rise of racism is what occasioned the resurgence of the racist in the mid-1970s? What is apparent is that the period 1973–1975 was the beginning of the deep recession cycles that narrowed the labor market and set the economy in a state of stagnation that produced a decrease in the national standard of living. The contraction of the job market since the mid-1970s has produced an atmosphere of severe competition among workers. The steady shift of manufacturing outside the shores of the United States is forcing thousands of blue-collar workers to accept lower wages, seek new occupations, or be without employment altogether. Unemployment has been at record levels over the past decade. Not since the Great Depression of the 1930s has a generation of young working-class whites faced a future in which many can expect to earn and own less than their parents. The farm region is also experiencing a long-term depression with record foreclosures on family farmers brought on by trade deficits and monopolization of agri-business and banks. This economic instability has produced a veritable sociological crisis for millions of working-class and farm families. They feel disavowed and disempowered.

In its 1980 annual report, the U.S. Justice Department makes the following observation (Walters, 1987):

> A factor for much of the racial and ethnic hostility was the perception by many white Americans that minorities, mainly blacks and Hispanics, were getting a better deal than anyone else, and that attention and continued effort to bring them into the mainstream threatened their welfare.

The ideology of the racist right focuses on the resentment felt in white communities. They orchestrate a "politics of resentment" by manipulating the issues of law and order, drugs, the death penalty, and affirmative action. In this climate, explicitly racist organizing has become widespread.

RACIAL CHANGE SINCE THE 1960s

As a result of the Civil Rights Act of 1964 and the Voting Rights Act of 1965, the decade of the 1960s was a time of significant change in race relations in the United States. Consequently, it is a good reference point from which to begin an examination of trends and developments in the status of African-Americans. However, because racial change has been uneven, it is not possible to concisely summarize its direction over the past two decades.

The greatest changes have taken place in the political sphere. Black mayors are leading—or have led—all of the largest cities in the United States; and they preside over many medium-sized cities as well. Although this has often entailed administering central cities burdened with well-nigh unsolvable problems within the context of a dominant white power structure, the new black political influence has also, on the plus side, democratized access to municipal and public service jobs.

The rise in black elected officials has been spectacular: The number increased from 280 in 1965 to 6,681 by 1987 (Boamah-Wiafe, 1990). Yet the fact that that figure represents less than 1.5% of all political officeholders shows that the degree of underrepresentation remains as significant as the gains (Joint Center for Political Studies, 1985).

Discrimination in jobs and training programs has definitely lessened over the past two decades. Yet racially exclusive practices still exist. Many small-sized firms (the fastest growing segment of the economy) exclude blacks and other minorities. And while affirmative action regulations constrain larger companies from such direct discrimination, ways are still found to ensure predominantly white work forces—for example, by avoiding areas of large black populations in the location of plants.

These economic developments have had adverse effects on the integrity and unity of the black community. The nuclear family has been weakened by joblessness and by the single-parent trend. The extended family is no longer strong enough to fill the gap as successfully as it did in the past. Drugs and crime also divide the community, creating a climate of fear and distrust. Even in street life there is less solidarity than in the past. The increasing distance between the classes makes it harder for the community to act with a unified voice. And integration, with all its positive features, has also weakened the traditional institutions of the black community: black businesses, black colleges, and even the black church.

Some observers have lamented what they call the "loss of African-American community." Some of this loss can be attributed to the economic bifurcation of the community and the resulting loss of community infrastructure. In addition, there has been a significant loss of black principals, vice-principals, guidance counselors, teachers, and coaches, as a result of school desegregation. Usually, desegregation has meant that blacks have moved into white-dominated institutions, and the schools they left have been reassigned to other purposes or closed. Seldom has it meant that whites integrated into institutions that have been traditionally black and where blacks held some of the power and influence.

CONCLUSION

Significant changes have occurred in the racial landscape of America during the past 30 years. However, the basic structural position of African-Americans is the same. Prospects for improving this situation may be significantly affected by impressions held by white Americans about the status of black Americans. Most whites believe that blacks are approaching parity in areas like housing, health care, employment, education, and treatment by the criminal justice system—a perception markedly different from that of most blacks.

In an NAACP Legal Defense Fund study (1989), more than two-thirds of blacks, as compared with one-third of whites, felt that blacks had fewer employment opportunities than whites of similar income and education. In answer to the question of whether blacks received equal pay for equal work, whites responded yes more than twice as often as blacks. Two-thirds of blacks felt that blacks had poorer housing and less access to housing, while only 41% of whites felt that way; twice as many whites as blacks thought that blacks were treated as well as whites by the criminal justice system. As the NAACP Legal Defense Fund study concluded, these gaps in perception—and between perception and reality—need to be addressed by the nation's leaders. These opposing views regarding the parity of blacks and whites in society present a significant impediment to racial progress.

NOTES

1. This section is based on W. Edwards (1988), Scientific Racism: Persistence and Change, *Trotter Institute Review, 2* (3), 14–18, published by the William Monroe Trotter Institute, University of Massachusetts, Boston.
2. Including the Southern Poverty Law Center, the Center for Democrats Renewal, the Klan Watch Network, the Joint Center for Political Studies, and the Newsletter on Racially Motivated Violence.

REFERENCES

Anderson, E. (1978). *A place on the corner.* Chicago: University of Chicago Press.

Baldwin, J. (1985). Lecture. First Baptist Church of America, Providence, RI.

Bell, D. A. (1980a). *Civil rights: Leading cases.* Boston: Little Brown.

Bell, D. A. (1980b). *Race, racism, and American law* (2nd ed.). Boston: Little Brown.

Bloom, J. M. (1987). *Class, race and the civil rights movement.* Bloomington, IN: Indiana University Press.

Blumer, H. (1958). Race prejudice as a sense of group position. *Pacific Sociological Review, 1*, 3–7.

Boamah-Wiafe, D. (1990). *The black experience in contemporary America.* Omaha: Wisdom Publications.

Bobo, L. (1983). Whites' opposition to busing: Symbolic racism or realistic group conflict? *Journal of Personality and Social Psychology, 45*, 1196–1210.

Brown v. Board of Education, 347 U.S. 483 (1954).

Clark, K. (1965). *Dark ghetto.* New York: Harper and Row.

Cross, T. L. (1984). *The black power imperative* (rev. ed.). New York: Faulkner Books.

Danielson, M. (1976). *The politics of exclusion.* New York: Columbia University Press.

Dolce, P. C. (Ed.). (1976). *Suburbia.* New York: Doubleday.

Dred Scott v. Sanford, 19 Howard 393 (60 U.S.)(1857).

Du Bois, W.E.B. (1961). *The souls of black folk.* Greenwich, CT: Fawcett. (Originally published 1903)

Du Bois, W.E.B. (1968). *Dusk of dawn: An essay toward an autobiography of race concept.* New York: Schocken Books. (Originally published 1940)

Ellison, R. (1964). *Shadow and act.* New York: Vintage.

Farley, R. (1970). The changing distribution of Negroes within metropolitan areas: The emergence of black suburbs. *American Journal of Sociology, 75*, 512–519.

Feagin, J. R., & Feagin, C. (1986). *Discrimination American style.* Malabar, FL: Krieger Publishing.

Hate and violence mark 1986. (1987, March). *The Monitor*, p. 1.

Himes, J. (1974). *Racial and ethnic relations.* Dubuque, IA: Brown.

Himes, J. (1987). Paper prepared for the Assessment of the Status of African-American Project, William Monroe Trotter Institute, University of Massachusetts, Boston.

Hofstadter, R. (1959). *Social Darwinism in American thought* (rev. ed.). New York: G. Braziller.

Joint Center for Political Studies. (1985). *Black elected officials: A national roster.* Washington, DC: Joint Center for Political Studies.

Jones v. Mayer, 392 U.S. 409 (1968).

Kinder, D. R., & Sears, D. D. (1991). Prejudice and politics: Symbolic racism versus racial threats to a good life. *Journal of Personality and Social Psychology, 40*, 414–431.

Levitan, S., et al. (1973). *Still a dream.* Washington, DC: Manpower and Policy Studies.

McConahay, J. B., & Hough, J. C. (1976). Symbolic racism. *Journal of Social Issues, 32*(2), 23–45.

NAACP Legal Defense Fund. (1989). *The unfinished agenda on race in America*. New York: Author.

National Committee Against Discrimination in Housing. (n.d.). *Guide to fair housing law enforcement*. Washington, DC: Author.

National Urban League. (1985). *The state of black America*. New York: Author.

Orfield, G. (1981). *Toward a strategy of urban integration: Lessons in school and housing policy from twelve cities*. New York: Ford Foundation.

Plessy v. Ferguson, 163 U.S. 537 (1896).

Reed, W. L. (1989). *African Americans and social policy in the 1990s* (Occasional Paper No. 17). Boston, MA: University of Massachusetts at Boston, William Monroe Trotter Institute.

Rodman, H. (1963). The lower class value stretch. *Social Forces*, *42*(2), 205–215.

Schuman, H., Steeh, C., & Bobo, L. (1985). *Racial attitudes in America: Trends and interpretations*. Cambridge, MA: Harvard University Press.

Schwendinger, H., & Schwendinger, J. (1974). *The sociologists of the chair*. New York: Basic Books.

Shelley v. Kraemer, 334 U.S. 1 (1948).

Smith, A. W. (1981). Tolerance of school desegregation, 1954–77. *Social Forces*, *59*, 1256–1274.

Smith, A. W. (1982). White attitudes towards residential integration. *Phylon*, *43*, 349–362.

Smith, A. W. (1985). Cohorts, education, and the evolution of tolerance. *Social Science Research*, *14*, 205–225.

Smith, A. W. (1988). Racial insularity at the core: Contemporary American racial attitudes. *Trotter Institute Review*, *2*(2), 9-14. Boston, MA: University of Massachusetts, William Monroe Trotter Institute.

Struyk, R. (1976). *Urban home ownership*. Lexington, MA: Lexington Books.

Swinton, D. H. (1990). Racial parity under laissez-faire: An impossible dream. In W. W. Van Horne and T. V. Tonnesen (Eds.), *Race: Twentieth century dilemmas—twenty-first century prognoses*. Madison, WI: University of Wisconsin, Institute on Race and Ethnicity.

Taeuber, K. E., & Taeuber, A. F. (1972). *Negroes in cities*. New York: Atheneum.

Taylor, W. L. (1984). Access to economic opportunity. In L. W. Dunbar (Ed.), *Minority report*. Pp. 26-57. New York: Pantheon.

U.S. Commission on Civil Rights. (1974). *Equal opportunity in suburbia*. Washington, DC: Government Printing Office.

U.S. Commission on Civil Rights. (1975). *Twenty years after Brown: Equal opportunity in housing*. Washington, DC: Government Printing Office.

U.S. Commission on Civil Rights. (1983). *A sheltered crisis: The state of fair housing in the eighties*. Washington, DC: Government Printing Office.

U.S. Department of Housing and Urban Development. (1979). *Measuring discrimination in American housing markets*. Washington, DC: Office of Policy Development and Research.

U.S. Department of Housing and Urban Development. (1984). *Recent evidence on discrimination in housing*. Washington, DC: Office of Policy Development and Research.

U.S. National Advisory Commission on Civil Disorders. (1968). *Report of the national commission on civil disorders*. New York: Bantam Books.

Walters, R. (1987, April). *White nationalism in America*. Paper presented at annual meeting of the African Heritage Studies Association, New York, NY.

Wilhelm, S. (1987). Paper prepared for the Assessment of the Status of African-Americans Project, William Monroe Trotter Institute, University of Massachusetts at Boston.

Wilkerson, I. (1990, May 9). Racial harassment altering blacks' choices on campus. *New York Times*, pp. 1, B10.

2

Race and Inequality in the Managerial Age

William Darity, Jr., with Jeremiah P. Cotton and Herbert Hill

> The Negro's prosperity today, limited as it is, is based upon the foundation laid by an alien race that is not disposed to go out of its way to prepare for the economic existence of anyone else but itself; therefore our present prosperity, as far as unemployment goes, is purely accidental. It is as accidental today as it was during the war of 1914–18 when colored men were employed in different occupations not because they were wanted, but because they were filling the places of men of other races who were not available at that time. Negroes are still filling places, and as time goes on and the age grows older our occupations will be gone from us, because those for whom we fill the places will soon appear, and as they do we shall gradually find our places among the millions of permanent unemployed.
>
> Marcus Garvey writing in the 1920s
> (Jacques-Garvey, 1969, vol. I, p. 48)

In 1970 Sidney Wilhelm published a provocative book entitled *Who Needs the Negro?* that advanced the thesis that a technological transformation toward automation in the United States would render blacks—first relied upon for their labor under slavery and thereafter as an industrial reserve—unnecessary. Wilhelm noted that European settlers temporarily needed native Americans upon arrival here to teach them crop techniques and to serve as allies against rival colonial powers. But in the postcolonial period the immigrant populations, who were soon to define the character of being "American," began to exterminate the natives. Wilhelm saw the same pattern developing for blacks in the late twentieth century.

In his review of Wilhelm's book, Lloyd Hogan (1972) complained:

> The [Wilhelm] theory is too vague and lacks the societal frame of reference correlated with a given configuration of technology. There is no definitive role assigned to the various social classes as these social classes emerge from, and acquire their characteristic signature from, the essential relations within the productive process. (p. 109)

Nearly two decades later, Wilhelm's disturbing thesis remains substantive, and its implications are unfolding with growing visibility. It also is now possible to meet Hogan's requirement for a more precise theory, to draw a sharp connection between the technological phenomenon Wilhelm depicted and the evolution of American social relations. Special attention must be given to the importance of the transition that has taken place from capitalist to managerial society, a transition from the dominance of the captains of industry and finance to the increasing dominance of the intellectuals and intelligentsia. The change is manifest in the authority given to experts in social analysis, policy-making, and management. Within this transition race and ethnicity continue to exercise decisive roles in dictating patterns of individual achievement and opportunity in the United States.

In particular, discrimination in its most encompassing sense continues to be operative. Although laws have been passed to make certain of such practices illegal, these laws have been largely circumvented, ignored, or gradually rolled back. In many instances the laws have not touched critical sites of discriminatory activity. To the extent that American society is intensely hierarchical, there is an incentive for members of ascriptively differentiated groups to coalesce and carve out occupational and status niches. Antidiscrimination laws certainly were not designed to level the hierarchical structure of U.S. society; hence the driving motive for discrimination as exclusion remains strong.

Alterations in the structure of the U.S. economy—associated with the social transformation from capitalism to managerialism—have meant that those with low skill levels have been barred from occupations where they once had access because of increased competition as these positions diminish or disappear. Discrimination, both anterior and interior to the point of employment, has also meant that large numbers of blacks are denied access to the newer occupations.

These are the circumstances that accompany justified concerns over the perpetuation of an American "underclass," disproportionately black, reproduced from generation to generation. This underclass is a consequence of social forces that are being unleashed as capitalism gives way to the managerial estate. These forces play out along the dimensions of class, race, and ethnicity, and they structure patterns of inequality in American society.

In addition to the persistent interracial gap between blacks and whites, there is also an intraracial gap in the circumstances of blacks themselves that also demands assessment. In a society with an increasingly bifurcated employment structure, where occupational growth is concentrated in low-wage, low-skilled jobs and in high-wage professional positions, the mass of blacks—to the extent that they find employment at all—are concentrated in the former set of jobs. This concentration aggravates the degree of polarization between the majority of blacks and the relatively small percentage of blacks who hold professional-level positions.

THE OPENING GAP

The gap between the general circumstances of the native black population of the United States (the descendants of Africans enslaved in the colonial era) and the native Indian population and the general circumstances of the nonblack majority (the descendants of Europeans who migrated to this continent) is multidimensional, reaching far beyond differences in economic well-being. The gap directly influences prospects for the health and well-being of upcoming generations, the sustenance of the spiritual and moral fiber of a people. The gap persists in the face of a host of changes: dramatic social policy initiatives such as the New Deal and the Great Society, the civil rights movement, periods of war and peace, and periods of prosperity and depression. The annual ritual of inspection of various statistical measures to assess the extent of black "progress"—undertaken, for example, in the National Urban League's annual publication *The State of Black America*—obscures the fundamental tenaciousness and pervasiveness of the gap. For even when such measures suggest changes in the absolute position of native blacks, they do not demonstrate over the long run any changes in the relative position.

Moreover, such statistical measures only scratch the surface of the deep gulf that exists between blacks and nonblacks in the United States. The narrow focus on indices of material well-being inhibits any serious analysis of the broad historical processes that have brought black America to its present position and continue to dictate its trajectory.

There is a deep contradiction in the economics literature of the late 1970s and early 1980s regarding the post–civil rights economic progress of black America. When examined carefully this contradiction indicates the opposing courses charted by the black underclass and the black middle class. For example, in 1973 Richard Freeman declared that there had been dramatic progress in the 1950s and especially in the 1960s, bringing blacks markedly closer to parity with whites in earnings. In fact, Freeman hypothesized that the trend toward "convergence in economic position . . . suggests a virtual collapse in traditional discriminatory patterns in the labor market" (p. 67). Freeman's declaration set the tone for a decade of research. But in 1986 Freeman set the tone for the next decade's research with a far more somber message:

> The 1970s witnessed severe economic plight among inner-city black youths that went beyond the worst predictions of even pessimistic social scientists. Rates of unemployment among young black men rose to unprecedented levels; their labor-force participation rates fell; and as a consequence their ratio of employment to population plummeted to extraordinarily low levels. (p. 353)

James Smith and Finis Welch (1989), while maintaining the position that blacks have made substantial strides economically over the past 40 years (due, they claim, to educational advance), conclude a recent paper with the following pessimistic note: "Unfortunately, there are also reasons for concern about the future, especially for the still large black underclass" (p. 561).

In 1973 Freeman's attention was drawn to the elite stratum of the black population and to evidence of its improved economic position, an improvement that directly led toward convergence in aggregate black-white earnings ratios. In 1983 Freeman's attention was drawn to the black underclass, whose economic position had stagnated, even deteriorated, since the civil rights revolution. In 1989 Smith and Welch see these two strata of the black population living economically disparate existences.

The intraracial gap is so visible and pressing that even black scholars who once stressed the homogeneity of the native black population now have shifted gears. In 1983 Kenneth Clark and John Hope Franklin introduced a Joint Center for Political Studies publication with the following observation: "At least three societies exist in America today: the mainstream, the assimilated minorities, and the excluded. These three societies are separate and unequal and the disparities between them threaten to destroy the national fabric" (p. 1). The black middle class, situated awkwardly among the "assimilated minorities," continues to dream of entering fully into "the mainstream." But the black underclass is too deeply situated among "the excluded" for such dreaming.

Freeman's 1973 reading of the aggregate data was peculiarly optimistic and inaccurate, but he was not alone in offering this rosy picture of the quickening pace of black economic progress. His claim in 1973 was that labor market discrimination against blacks had been all but eliminated as a result of government antidiscrimination legislation and enforcement of affirmative action in hiring. Other scholars took the position that discrimination in labor markets could not persist anyway, regardless of government action, since the "natural" forces of competition would eliminate such discrimination, leaving only individual productivity differences as the basic explanation for racial inequality along wage-earning lines.[1] Whether it was government action or private action that was eliminating discrimination, all scholars agreed that the alleged decline in discrimination pointed toward improvement in the black condition. They then sought to quantify this improvement.[2]

Most of the good news emanating from these sources has been narrowly based, centering mainly on movements in black-white male wage and income ratios. Smith and Welch jubilantly proclaimed in 1986 that "[in 1940] the typical black male worker earned only 43% as much as his white counterpart. By 1980 the average black man in the labor force earned 73% as much as the typical white man" (p. 1). And although these wage gains were particularly substantial for black males with less than ten years of work experience, they were enjoyed as well by all other categories.

All of this is consistent with the Smith-Welch "vintage" hypothesis that predicts that better-educated young black males entering the labor market and replacing older, less well-educated blacks will, over time, accelerate the rate of convergence of black-white skills and hence black-white male wages. Indeed, in terms of quantity of schooling measured by median years, the racial gap has closed (see Table 2.1). But the question remains: Does that translate into lessening of differences in income, opportunity, health, and well-being?

It should go without say that the economic situation of native blacks as a whole can in no way be sufficiently represented by shifts in the income and earnings of black males relative to white males. There are other important indicators that must be considered in order to portray the past and present economic conditions of blacks. But even the picture in regard to black male income and earnings has clouded over since the 1970s. Bradbury and Browne (1986) have adduced evidence that shows not only a decline in the black-white male median income ratio since 1978, but also an apparent breakdown in the much-vaunted vintage effect.

Table 2.2 is an expanded and somewhat modified version of the Bradbury and Browne data. It can be seen there that the black-white median

Table 2.1
Median Years of Schooling of Head for Families with Head 25 Years Old and Older, by Poverty Status and Race of Head, 1970–1984[a]

	Male Head				Female Head			
	Below Poverty		Total		Below Poverty		Total	
Year	Black	White	Black	White	Black	White	Black	White
1984	10.6[b]	12.1	12.3	12.7	11.6	12.0	12.2	12.5
1981	9.4	11.5	12.2	12.7	11.4	12.0	12.1	12.4
1980	9.3	11.1	12.1	12.6	11.1	11.9	12.0	12.6
1979	8.8	10.4	12.1	12.6	11.1	11.6	12.0	12.4
1978	8.7	10.5	12.2	12.6	11.0	11.8	11.8	12.3
1977	8.5	10.0	12.0	12.6	10.8	11.6	11.6	12.3
1976	8.7	10.3	11.7	12.5	10.5	11.4	11.4	52.2
1975	7.9	9.4	11.1	12.5	10.5	10.8	11.2	12.2
1974	7.2	9.6	10.9	12.5	10.4	10.7	11.0	12.2
1973	7.2	8.9	10.6	12.4	10.1	11.1	10.7	12.1
1972	8.1	8.9	10.6	12.4	10.1	10.8	10.7	12.1
1971	7.2	8.8	10.2	12.3	9.9	10.4	10.3	12.1
1970	6.8	8.7	10.0	12.3	9.3	10.5	10.1	12.1

[a]Data in this series are unavailable between 1982 and 1983.
[b]In 1984, half of black male householders whose families had incomes below the poverty level had less than 10.6 years of schooling and half had more.
Source of data: U.S. Bureau of Census, *Current Population Reports, Consumer Income,* Series P-60, No. 81, pp. 83-84; No. 86, pp. 113-114; No. 91, pp. 113-114; No. 98, pp. 117-118; No. 102, p. 105; No. 105, p. 132; No. 115, p. 135; No. 119, p. 133; No. 124, p. 145; No. 130, p. 140; No. 133, p. 128; No. 149, pp. 28, 29. March 1982, *Current Population Survey* (unpublished data), pp. 390, 392, 400, 398, 416, 414, 424, 422.

Table 2.2

Black-White Male Median Income Ratios for Year-Round, Fully Employed Workers, by Age Cohorts, 1967–1987

Year	All Ages[a]	20-24	25-34 Total	25-29	30-34	35-44 Total	35-39	40-44	45-54	55-64
1967	.64	.68	.73	n.a.	n.a.	.61	n.a.	n.a.	.65	.57
1968	.68	.77	.71	n.a.	n.a.	.63	n.a.	n.a.	.68	.64
1969	.66	.80	.70	n.a.	n.a.	.66	n.a.	n.a.	.66	.62
1970	.68	.77	.72	n.a.	n.a.	.65	n.a.	n.a.	.67	.67
1971	.68	.86	.73	n.a.	n.a.	.63	n.a.	n.a.	.66	.60
1972	.68	.81	.72	n.a.	n.a.	.65	n.a.	n.a.	.63	.66
1973	.67	.79	.76	n.a.	n.a.	.68	n.a.	n.a.	.64	.62
1974	.70	.79	.80	n.a.	n.a.	.71	n.a.	n.a.	.67	.64
1975	.73	.83	.80	.85	.75	.72	.75	.69	.68	.71
1976	.72	.81	.79	.81	.76	.69	.70	.68	.66	.66
1977	.69	.84	.75	.77	.76	.74	.72	.75	.69	.60
1978	.77	.72	.86	.90	.84	.77	.81	.74	.69	.69
1979	.73	.79	.78	.77	.80	.76	.77	.75	.65	.66
1980	.70	.83	.76	.76	.78	.71	.70	.73	.64	.65
1981	.71	.82	.78	.82	.76	.68	.66	.69	.61	.66
1982	.71	.82	.77	.74	.79	.69	.73	.65	.64	.67
1983	.71	.74	.75	.75	.75	.76	.80	.75	.67	.60
1984	.68	.80	.72	.69	.73	.76	.82	.69	.67	.60
1985	.70	.79	.73	.69	.70	.70	.72	.69	.68	.68
1986	.71	.76	.73	.71	.73	.73	.73	.73	.71	.61
1987	.71	.79	.71	.75	.69	.76	.75	.78	.66	.65

[a]Includes persons 14 years and older in 1967-1978, and 15 years and older in 1979-1987.
Source: U.S. Bureau of Census, *Current Population Reports*, Series P-60, Money Income of Households, Families and Persons in the United States, various years.

income ratio for fully employed males of all ages rose from .64 in 1967 to a high of .77 in 1978 and then fell to .68 in 1984. The incomes of younger black males, those 20 to 34 years of age, were generally higher relative to their white counterparts than those of older black males. The "average" black-white income ratio for 20- to 24-year-olds over 18-year period was slightly over .79, while that for 25- to 34-year-olds was around .76. For 35- to 44-year-olds the average over the period was .69; for 45- to 54-year-olds it was .65; and for 55- to 64-year-olds it was .64. In accord with the expectations of the vintage hypothesis, younger blacks in the late 1960s with higher relative incomes than older cohorts were able to improve or at least maintain their relative income position over the next ten years.

In Table 2.3, changes in the income ratios of various cohorts over ten-year time spans are shown. The 20- to 24-year-old cohorts of 1967 to 1970, and the 25- to 34-year-old cohorts of 1967 to 1969 either improved or held to their relative income positions over the next ten years. After 1980, however, as Bradbury and Browne state, "this positive ripple effect broke down" (1986, p. 34). With but one exception the relative incomes of the 20- to 24-year-old and 25- to 34-year-old cohorts of 1971 to 1974 had decreased ten years later over the 1981 to 1984 period. Black male workers who were 35 years and older in the late 1960s and mid-1970s also fared poorly over the next ten years. With but few exceptions their relative incomes were lower ten years later.

The ten-year span for the 20- to 24-year-old cohorts from 1970 to 1974 can be divided into two five-year periods. The slight increase in the relative income of the 20- to 24-year-old cohort between 1970 and 1980 was composed of a sharp rise between 1970 and 1975 and an almost equally sharp decline between 1975 and 1980. The 1973 cohort experienced an even steeper rise in their relative incomes between 1973 and 1978 and an even greater decline between 1978 and 1983. Nor were the 1980s kind to the 30- to 34-year-old and 35- to 39-year-old cohorts over the five-year spans beginning in 1975. The general picture suggested by this data does not support the predictions of those who argued that the wage gains experienced by black males in the late 1960s and early 1970s would be maintained throughout their work careers. Life-cycle "gains" are not borne out by the data.

Matters are further complicated by the fact that the basis for the numbers in Tables 2.2 and 2.3 is a rather selective one and does not reflect the full reality of white male–black male income disparities. The data in Tables 2.2 and 2.3 are based on year-round, full-time workers, and such workers among blacks are a smaller proportion of all income recipients than they

Table 2.3
Changes in Black-White Male Median Income Ratios Over Various Time Spans, by Selected Age Cohorts, 1967–1987

	10-Year Span			
Year	20-24	Year	30-34	Direction of change in ratios over time span
1967	.68	1977	.76	increase
1968	.77	1978	.84	increase
1969	.80	1979	.80	unchanged
1970	77	1980	.78	increase
1971	.86	1981	.81	decrease
1972	.81	1982	.79	decrease
1973	.79	1983	.73	decrease
1974	.79	1984	.73	decrease
1975	.83	1985	.69	decrease
1976	.81	1986	.71	decrease
1977	.84	1987	.69	decrease

	10-Year Span			
Year	25-34	Year	35-44	Direction of change in ratios over time span
1967	.73	1977	.74	increase
1968	.71	1978	.77	increase
1969	.70	1979	.76	increase
1970	.72	1980	.71	decrease
1971	.73	1981	.68	decrease
1972	.72	1982	.69	decrease
1973	.76	1983	.76	unchanged
1974	.80	1984	.76	decrease
1975	.80	1985	.70	decrease
1976	.79	1986	.73	decrease
1977	.75	1987	.76	increase

	10-Year Span			
Year	35-44	Year	45-54	Direction of change in ratios over time span
1967	.61	1977	.59	decrease
1968	.63	1978	.69	increase
1969	.66	1979	.65	decrease
1970	.65	1980	.64	decrease
1971	.63	1981	.63	decrease
1972	.65	1982	.64	decrease
1973	.68	1983	.67	decrease
1974	.71	1984	.67	decrease
1975	.72	1985	.68	decrease
1976	.69	1986	.71	increase
1977	.74	1987	.66	decrease

	10-Year Span			
Year	45-54	Year	55-64	Direction of change in ratios over time span
1967	.65	1977	.60	decrease
1968	.68	1978	.69	increase

Table 2.3 (continued)

Year	10-Year Span 45-54	Year	55-64	Direction of change in ratios over time span
1969	.68	1979	.65	unchanged
1970	.67	1980	.60	decrease
1971	.66	1981	.66	unchanged
1972	.63	1982	.67	increase
1973	.64	1983	.60	decrease
1974	.67	1984	.60	decrease
1975	.68	1985	.68	unchanged
1976	.66	1986	.61	decrease
1977	.59	1987	.65	increase

Year	5-Year Span 20-24	Year	25-29	Year	30-34
1970	.77	1975	.85	1980	.78
1971	.86	1976	.81	1981	.76
1972	.81	1977	.77	1982	.79
1973	.79	1978	.90	1983	.73
1974	.79	1979	.77	1984	.73
1975	.83	1980	.76	1985	.69
1976	.81	1981	.82	1986	.71
1977	.84	1982	.74	1987	.69
1978	.72	1983	.75		
1979	.79	1984	.69		
1980	.83	1985	.77		
1981	.82	1986	.73		
1982	.82	1987	.75		

Year	5-Year Span 30-34	Year	35-39	Direction of change in ratios over time span
1975	.75	1980	.70	decrease
1976	.76	1981	.66	decrease
1977	.76	1982	.73	decrease
1978	.84	1983	.80	decrease
1979	.80	1984	.82	increase
1980	.78	1985	.72	decrease
1981	.76	1986	.73	decrease
1982	.79	1987	.75	decrease

Year	5-Year Span 30-39	Year	40-44	Direction of change in ratios over time span
1975	.69	1980	.73	increase
1976	.70	1981	.69	decrease
1977	.82	1982	.65	decrease
1978	.81	1983	.75	decrease
1979	.77	1984	.69	decrease
1980	.70	1985	.69	decrease
1981	.66	1986	.73	increase
1982	.73	1987	.78	increase

Source: See table 2-2.

Table 2.4
Year-Round, Full-Time Workers as a Percent of All Workers, 1967–1987

Year	Black Males	White Males	Black Females	White Females
1967	53.0%	61.5%	31.8%	31.7%
1968	53.0	61.1	31.2	31.0
1969	51.7	59.9	30.0	30.8
1970	50.0	57.3	30.6	29.9
1971	48.4	57.3	29.6	30.5
1972	50.8	58.2	32.8	30.3
1973	50.5	58.7	31.3	30.0
1974	46.7	56.9	30.4	30.3
1975	43.3	54.1	29.2	28.6
1976	45.2	54.1	29.7	28.5
1977	46.3	54.5	30.4	29.2
1978	45.0	55.9	31.4	28.8
1979	46.8	56.1	30.3	27.5
1980	43.8	55.0	31.4	27.9
1981	45.2	53.9	31.0	28.0
1982	41.5	51.9	32.0	28.3
1983	43.9	52.7	33.2	29.6
1984	44.8	54.9	35.0	30.3
1985	47.5	55.3	35.7	31.0
1986	46.4	55.3	35.3	31.8
1987	48.5	56.5	36.4	32.9

Source: See table 2-2.

are among whites. Moreover, while the proportion of full-time male workers has been declining for both groups, the decline in absolute terms for blacks has been greater than that for whites. In 1967, as Table 2.4 shows, 53% of black male workers worked full-time year-round, while for white workers the figures was 61.5%. By 1987 the black male proportion was about 5 percentage points lower, and the white male proportion was down 5 percentage points to 56.5%. The lowest point was 41.5% for black males and 51.9% for white males during 1982.

A more telling measure is the income ratio for all workers, both full- and part-time and full- and part-year. A comparison of the data in Table 2.5 and that in Table 2.2 shows that the absolute values of the median income ratios for all workers are lower than they are for full-time workers. Between 1967 and 1974, the average difference between the two ratios for workers of all ages was around 8%. Between 1975 and 1987 the average difference increased to around 12%. None of this affects the conclusions reached with respect to the decline in black relative incomes by age cohorts over the 1980s. Whether we use full-time data or part-time data the decline is still there.

A measure closer still to the economic reality of black males is that adopted by Darity (1980; Darity & Myers, 1980), who included not only those with income but those without as well. This requires us to use mean

Table 2.5
Black-White Male Median Income Ratios for All Workers, by Age Cohorts, 1967–1987

Year	All Ages[a]	20-24	25-34	35-44	45-54	55-64
1967	.57	.71	.72	.56	.57	.53
1968	.59	.83	.70	.62	.63	.53
1969	.58	.91	.65	.62	.57	.56
1970	.59	.80	.65	.62	.61	.55
1971	.60	.78	.68	.58	.61	.54
1972	.61	.82	.70	.60	.60	.48
1973	.61	.84	.71	.61	.57	.53
1974	.61	.77	.74	.64	.55	.53
1975	.60	.81	.73	.63	.53	.53
1976	.60	.76	.69	.64	.56	.53
1977	.59	.78	.70	.66	.53	.52
1978	.60	.68	.73	.70	.61	.51
1979	.63	.75	.72	.63	.56	.51
1980	.60	.71	.68	.61	.56	.49
1981	.60	.76	.70	.66	.56	.47
1982	.60	.61	.71	.62	.56	.50
1983	.58	.54	.65	.66	.62	.52
1984	.57	.69	.60	.63	.60	.47
1985	.63	.62	.69	.64	.63	.53
1986	.60	.61	.65	.65	.62	.54
1987	.59	.63	.65	.66	.56	.51

[a]Includes persons 14 years and older in 1967-1978, and 15 years and older in 1979-1987.
Source: See table 2-2.

rather than median as the measure of average and to correct it for those who have been excluded because they had no income.[3] This simple correction involves multiplying the mean by the proportion of the population with income. Such a result is presented in Table 2.6. The proportion of black males with income declined slightly over the 1967–1987 period, while the proportion of whites with income increased. In contrast to the median income ratios in Table 2.2, the mean income ratios are uniformly lower and the "corrected" mean income ratios lower still. Once again, the story is the same with respect to progress in this ratio. While the ratio for fully employed workers was higher in 1987 than in 1967 (.71 versus .64), and the ratio for all workers also was higher in 1987 than in 1967 (.59 versus .57), the mean income ratio for those with and without income was an identical .55 in both years.

Expected payoffs in income relative to increased black male educational attainment also hit a snag during the 1980s. As Table 2.7 shows, the black-white median income ratios for males 25 years and older in all schooling classes rose in the late 1960s and early 1970s. During the 1980s, however, the rates declined for all except those with four or more years of college. The decline was particularly pronounced among black high school graduates, whose income relative to whites was the same in 1987 as in

Table 2.6

Mean Income for Males with and without Income, 1967–1987

Year	Mean Income	Approximate Share	Black Mean Income	White Mean Income	Approximate Share	Corrected White Mean Income	Black-White Income Ratio	Corrected Black-White Income Ratio
1967	$ 3,696	.88	$ 3,260	$ 6,414	.93	$ 5,956	.59	.55
1968	4,018	.89	3,559	6,895	.93	6,407	.59	.56
1969	4,361	.88	3,857	7,508	.93	6,984	.58	.55
1970	4,683	.86	4,027	7,840	.93	7,273	.60	.55
1971	4,888	.86	4,182	8,203	.92	7,583	.60	.55
1972	5,447	.84	4,572	8,980	.93	8,318	.61	.55
1973	5,864	.86	5,057	9,652	.93	9,004	.61	.56
1974	6,210	.85	5,263	10,083	.93	9,420	.62	.56
1975	6,633	.84	5,549	10,832	.93	10,025	.61	.55
1976	7,180	.84	6,034	11,604	.93	10,836	.62	.56
1977	7,743	.84	6,513	12,537	.93	11,659	.62	.56
1978	8,541	.86	7,307	13,609	.93	12,839	.63	.57
1979	9,383	.88	8,279	14,920	.96	14,376	.63	.58
1980	9,843	.87	8,607	15,967	.96	15,299	.62	.56
1981	10,531	.87	9,119	17,195	.96	16,507	.61	.55
1982	11,050	.83	9,199	18,071	.95	17,201	.61	.53
1983	11,501	.84	9,716	18,823	.95	17,941	.61	.54
1984	12,119	.86	10,409	20,259	.96	19,367	.60	.54
1985	13,376	.87	11,678	21,523	.96	20,569	.62	.57
1986	13,861	.87	12,124	22,746	.96	21,749	.61	.56
1987	14,391	.87	12,500	23,643	.96	22,691	.61	.55

Source: See table 2-2.

Table 2.7
Black-White Male Median Income Ratios, by Educational Attainment, Persons 25 Years and Older, Selected Years

Year	Elementary 0-8 Years	Some HighSchool 9-11 years	High School Grad 12 year	Total College 13+years	Some College 13-15 years	College Plus 16+years
1964	.67	.68	.66	.66	n.a.	n.a.
1969	.73	.71	.71	.69	.74	.69
1974	.68	.74	.76	.73	.78	.71
1980	.63	.76	.73	.70	.74	.71
1984	.68	.71	.66	.69	.74	.71
1985	.67	.80	.74	.68	.71	.77
1986	.63	.81	.71	.70	.77	.73
1987	.73	.71	.66	.70	.77	.73

Source: See table 2-2.

Table 2.8
Black-White Median Family Income, in 1984 Dollars, 1967–1984

Year	Black Median Income	White Median Income	White-Black Median Income Difference	Black-White Median Income Ratio
1967	$15,166	$25,616	$10,450	.59
1968	16,003	26,682	10,659	.60
1969	16,997	27,750	10,753	.61
1970	16,596	27,381	10,585	.61
1971	16,517	27,371	10,854	.60
1972	17,042	28,674	11,632	.59
1973	16,990	29,439	12,449	.58
1974	16,863	28,241	11,378	.60
1975	16,943	27,536	10,593	.62
1976	16,863	28,349	11,486	.60
1977	16,391	28,693	12,302	.57
1978	17,321	29,244	11,923	.59
1979	16,562	29,248	12,686	.57
1980	15,976	27,611	11,635	.58
1981	15,151	26,858	11,707	.56
1982	14,633	26,475	11,482	.55
1983	15,181	26,937	11,756	.56
1984	15,431	27,686	12,255	.56

Source: See table 2-1.

1964. It would appear from this data that the relative income gains associated with increased educational attainments made by black males during the 1960s and 1970s have eroded in the 1980s.

Finally, we consider measures of the relative resources available to the black family. Two such measures, median family income and family wealth and asset ownership, also belie the claims of "dramatic" black economic advances. In 1967, as Table 2.8 shows, the average black family had an income of $15,166 (in 1984 dollars) available to it, whereas the average white family enjoyed an income that was $10,450 higher at $25,616. Thus for every $1 of white family income, black families had 59 cents. By 1984 the gap had grown wider. Black median family income in 1984 was $15,431, some $12,255 less than the $27,686 white families received. In that year, for every $1 of white family income, black families had 56 cents. Moreover, white families fared much better than blacks in terms of real income growth. The black 1984 median family income was just $265 higher than the 1967 income; whites, on the other hand, enjoyed an increase of $2,070 over their 1967 income. And while black family income rose between 1967 and 1978, when it peaked at $17,321, so also did the difference rise between the amount of income available to whites and to blacks. This difference reached its peak in 1979 at $12,686. After 1978 and 1979, both black and white real income started to decline, but black income declined faster.

If one wishes to take a slightly longer view of racial income comparisons, one must use the "black and other races" category. Data on relative median family income for this category goes back to 1947. Although blacks make up the overwhelming majority of the families in this category, the income disparity between blacks and the other groups such as Chinese and Japanese is such that it lends a considerable upward bias to the ratio. In Table 2.9, the two income ratios are presented and contrasted. It not only shows the degree of divergence between the two statistics, but also indicates that there has been an increase in this divergence over time. The 1967–1987 interval seems to be composed of two distinct periods. From 1967 to 1976 the average difference between the two ratios was 2.9%; but from 1977 to 1984 the difference almost doubled to 5.4%. It might be inferred from this that the other races in the category have been making substantial economic gains relative to blacks since 1977. However, even if one relied solely on the black-and-other/white ratio, things still would not look very rosy. The black-and-other/white ratio hovered between .51 and .57 from the 1940s into the mid-1960s. Then it rose fitfully over the late 1960s and reached its peak of .65 in 1975. It has since headed downward and has been stuck at around .62 throughout the 1980s.

It is of interest to note how black relative family incomes have fared under different federal administrations. In Table 2.10 such a comparison is made. Black family income was highest on average during the two Ford years, while the next highest period was during the six-year Nixon regime. Black relative family income was at its lowest during the first four Reagan years. During that time black families had on average $1,800 less in yearly income than they did during the Ford years. The story is exactly the same

Table 2.9
Comparison of Black and Other Races, White Median Family Income Ratios and Black-White Median Family Income Ratios, 1947–1987

Year	Black & Other Races-White Ratio	Black-White Ratio	Year	Black & Other Races-White Ratio	Black-White Ratio	Difference Between Ratios
1947	.51	n.a.	1967	.62	.59	.03
1948	.53	n.a.	1968	.63	.60	.03
1949	.51	n.a.	1969	.63	.61	.02
1950	.54	n.a.	1970	.64	.61	.03
1951	.53	n.a.	1971	.63	.60	.03
1952	.57	n.a.	1972	.62	.59	.03
1953	.56	n.a.	1973	.60	.58	.02
1954	.56	n.a.	1974	.64	.60	.04
1955	.55	n.a.	1975	.65	.62	.03
1956	.53	n.a.	1976	.63	.60	.03
1957	.54	n.a.	1977	.61	.57	.04
1958	.51	n.a.	1978	.64	.59	.05
1959	.52	n.a.	1979	.61	.57	.04
1960	.55	n.a.	1980	.63	.58	.05
1961	.53	n.a.	1981	.62	.56	.06
1962	.53	n.a.	1982	.62	.55	.07
1963	.53	n.a.	1983	.62	.56	.06
1964	.56	n.a.	1984	.62	.56	.05
1965	.55	n.a.	1985	.64	.58	.06
1966	.60	n.a.	1986	.63	.57	.06
			1987	.63	.56	.07

Source: See table 2-2.

Table 2.10
Median Family Income During the Last Eight Administrations, in 1984 Dollars

Administration[a]	Black Median Income	Black & Other Median Income	White Median Income	Black-White Ratio	Black & Other Races-White Ratio
Truman 1947-52	n.a.	$ 7,944	$14,907	n.a.	.53
Eisenhower 1953-60	n.a.	10,064	18,693	n.a.	.54
Kennedy 1961-63	n.a.	11,421	21,466	n.a.	.53
Johnson 1964-66	n.a.	13,671	23,961	n.a.	.57
Johnson 1967-68	15,585	16,269	26,149	.60	.62
Nixon 1969-74	16,868	17,609	28,143	.60	.63
Ford 1975-76	16,903	17,955	27,943	.61	.64
Carter 1977-80	16,563	17,825	28,699	.58	.62
Reagan 1981-84	15,099	16,710	26,989	.56	.62

[a]Income figures are averages over the indicated years.
Source: Data from *Economic Report of the President*
Washington, DC: Government Printing Office.

Table 2.11
Distribution of Family, by Family Type, for Selected Years, 1973–1987

Year	Total	Black Married Couple Family	White Married Couple Family	Black Female-Headed Family	White Female-Headed Family
1973	100%	61.8%	87.7%	34.0%	9.9%
1974	100	60.9	86.9	35.3	10.5
1975	100	60.0	86.8	35.9	10.8
1976	100	58.7	86.7	37.1	10.9
1977	100	56.1	85.9	39.2	11.5
1979	100	55.5	85.6	40.5	11.6
1980	100	53.7	85.1	41.7	11.9
1981	100	55.1	84.5	40.6	12.4
1983	100	51.6	84.4	43.1	12.6
1984	100	51.2	83.9	43.7	12.8
1985	100	53.2	83.5	41.5	12.9
1986	100	52.7	83.4	41.8	13.0
1987	100	51.3	83.2	42.8	12.9

Source: See table 2-2.

for the median income of blacks and other races during the 1967–1984 period, only the numbers are slightly higher.

White family incomes also fell under Reagan. White families' average median income of $26,989 was the second lowest since the 1967–1968 Johnson years. Given their loyalties in the 1980 presidential election, it is ironic that their best income performance took place during the preceding Carter administration.

Undoubtedly one of the major reasons average black family income is as low as it is, is because of the large and increasing proportion of black female–headed families, an issue we will return to below. Table 2.11 shows that in 1973, 34% of all black families were headed by a female, while nearly 62% were husband-wife. This compares to 10% white female–headed and nearly 88% white husband-wife families. By 1987 black female–headed families represented almost 43% of all black families, and married couple families were down to 51%. White female–headed families had also risen by 1987 to about 13%, and white married families had fallen somewhat to 83%.

Thus if, as in Table 2.12, we consider only married-couple families, the black-white median family income ratios improve considerably in percentage terms, although the trend in the last eight or nine years has been quite flat.

One would expect black married-couple families to do better relative to white families than black families taken as a whole not only because of the presence of a high number of black female–headed families but also

Table 2.12
Black-White Median Family Income Ratios, by Family Type, Selected Years, 1973–1987

Year	Black-White Married Couple Income Ratio	Black-White Female Head Income Ratio	Black Female Head/White Married Couple Income Ratio	White Female Head/White Married Couple Income Ratio	Black Female Head/Black Married Couple Income Ratio
1973[a]	.72	.64	.32	.50	.44
1974[a]	.74	.61	.32	.52	.43
1975[a]	.76	.64	.33	.51	.43
1976[a]	.78	.62	.31	.50	.39
1977[a]	.75	.64	.31	.49	.42
1979[a]	.77	.60	.32	.53	.41
1980[b]	.79	.62	.32	.51	.40
1981[b]	.77	.60	.30	.49	.38
1983[b]	.79	.58	.29	.50	.37
1984[b]	.78	.57	.29	.50	.37
1985[b]	.78	.59	.29	.50	.38
1986[b]	.80	.59	.28	.47	.35
1987[b]	.77	.57	.28	.48	.36

[a]Family heads 14 years and older
[b]Family heads 15 years and older
Source: See table 2-2.

Table 2.13
Black-White Working Wives in Married-Couple Families, by Percentage, Selected Years, 1973–1987

Year	Black Wives in Labor Force	White Wives in Labor Force
1973	51.5%	40.7%
1974	53.5	42.3
1975	56.8	43.0
1976	56.8	44.4
1977	58.0	45.2
1979	59.1	48.4
1980	59.6	49.3
1981	59.8	49.4
1983	63.3	51.3
1984	64.0	52.5
1985	64.1	52.9
1986	65.4	54.3
1987	65.8	55.3

Source: See table 2-2.

because of the high relative proportion of black working wives in black married-couple families.

As shown in Table 2.13, in 1973 nearly 52% of the wives in black married-couple families worked compared to 41% of their while counterparts. By 1987 the proportion of black working wives had increased to 66%, while that of white working wives had increased to 55%.

The relative penury of the black female–headed family is revealed in the differential between their incomes and those of white and black married-couple families, as well as white female–headed families. With respect to the latter, in 1973 a black family headed by a female had only 64% as much income on average as a similar white family. By 1987 this was down to 57%. In 1973 a black female–headed family had only 32% as much income as a white married-couple family; by 1987 this was down to 28%. In both 1973 and 1984, a white female–headed family had about half as much income as a white married-couple family. Among blacks, in 1973, a black female-headed family had 44% as much income as a black married-couple family; by 1987 the proportion had fallen to 36%.

Thus, with nearly half of all black families headed by a female and with the average income of such families less than a third that available to white married-couple families, it is difficult to be upbeat about the economic condition of the black family, the most important center of black life.

While there is not a great deal of comparative data on family wealth and asset ownership, what little there is tells an even more dismal tale about the relative economic plight of black families than does the income comparison. Table 2.14 reproduces census data on net worth and asset ownership. According to the census study, net worth is defined as the value of interest-earning assets (such as savings accounts, money-market deposit accounts, certificates of deposit, interest-earning checking accounts, money-market funds, corporate and municipal bonds, U.S. government securities), stocks and mutual fund shares, residential and rental property, vacation homes and land holdings, a business or profession, mortgages held by sellers, and motor vehicles, less liabilities in the form of any debts secured by any asset, credit cards, store bills, bank loans, or other unsecured debts.

According to the data displayed in Table 2.14, in 1984 the median net worth of a black family was approximately $3,400, while that of a white family was almost 12 times as much at approximately $39,000. Another way to look at it is that for every $1 in wealth held by a white family, a comparable black family had 9 cents in wealth. For those families with incomes under $11,000 (the "official" poverty population), white families had 96 times greater net worth than blacks. White families with incomes

Table 2.14
Median Families Net Worth, 1984

Net Worth by Income	Black	White	Black-White Ratio	White-Black Ratio
Median Net Worth (All Households)	$3,397	$39,135	.09	11.52
Less than $10,800	88	8,443	.01	95.94
$10,800 to $23,999	4,218	30,514	.14	7.28
$24,000 to $45,999	15,977	50,529	.32	3.16
$48,000 plus	58,758	128,237	.46	2.18

Median Net Worth, by Family Type, 1984

Family Type	Black	White	Black-White Ratio	White-Black Ratio
Married-Couple Families	$13,061	$54,184	.24	4.15
Female-Headed Families	671	22,500	.03	33.53

Source: U. S. Bureau of Census, *Current Population Reports,* Series P-70, No. 7, Household Wealth and Asset Ownership: 1984, Table G, p. 5.

between $11,000 and $48,000 (the broad middle class) had 3 to 7 times more wealth than their black counterparts. White families with incomes in excess of $48,000 had twice the wealth of blacks in that category.

The breakdown by family type shows that white married-couple families had four times more wealth than black married-couple families; and white female–headed families had nearly 34 times more wealth than black female–headed families. White female–headed families on average had greater net worth than black married-couple families.

Blacks and whites also diverge when it comes to the composition of asset ownership. According to the census study, white householders, when compared to black householders, held a greater percentage of their net worth in durable goods such as housing (65% versus 41%) and motor vehicles (11% versus 6%), and a lower percentage in financial assets such as stocks and mutual fund shares (1% versus 7%) and deposits at financial institutions (7% versus 15%) (U.S. Bureau of the Census, 1983b).

Much is often made of the narrow gap in black and white female income and earnings as evidence for the healthy state of the black economy (see Table 2.15). The black-white female median income ratios for year-round, full-time workers in all age groups increased over the 1967 to 1984 period. In 1967 a typical black female full-time worker had an income that was

Table 2.15
Black-White Female Median Income Ratios for Year-Round, Full-Time Workers, by Age Cohorts, 1967–1984

Year	All Ages[a]	20-24	25-34	35-44	45-54	55-64
1967	.75	.81	.76	.75	.72	.58
1968	.76	.83	.79	.76	.74	.61
1969	.80	.83	.81	.86	.70	.70
1970	.82	.93	.87	.86	.71	.60
1971	.88	.99	.92	.88	.84	.70
1972	.86	.95	.86	.83	.82	.72
1973	.85	.88	.89	.80	.80	.72
1974	.91	.96	.94	.89	.83	.79
1975	.96	.99	.97	.93	.87	.73
1976	.94	.99	.93	.93	.87	.75
1977	.94	.96	.91	.93	.91	.74
1978	.93	.96	.92	.88	.97	.77
1979	.92	1.00	.90	.94	.88	.79
1980	.93	.95	.93	.90	.94	.84
1981	.90	.88	.92	.82	.88	.80
1982	.89	.92	.94	.88	.82	.77
1983	.89	.88	.84	.94	.87	.74
1984	.90	.89	.86	.97	.90	.86

[a]Includes persons 14 years and older in 1967-1978, and 15 years and older in 1979-1984
Source: See table 2-1.

75% of the income of a similarly placed white female. By 1984 her income was 90% as much. Indeed, in 1979, 20- to 24-year-old black women reached parity with white women. And although there was a general decline in the income ratios of younger women over the mid- to late-1970s, they are still in a better position vis-à-vis white women than black men are relative to white men.

However, in measuring the incomes of black women against those of white women one needs to deal with a much more significant background: the fact that both groups are at a disadvantage in the labor market, that both groups receive substandard incomes. Measuring the progress of one solely in terms of the other gives an incomplete and misleading picture of the economic conditions of each.

A more instructive approach is that taken in Table 2.16, where incomes of both black females and white females are compared with those of white males, the benchmark group. Median income ratios are presented both for all workers and a year-round, full-time workers. Mean income ratios (such as those for males in Table 2.6), corrected to include persons without income, are also shown. The latter ratios and those for all workers are quite similar.

While all three statistics show that both black- and white-female incomes relative to those of white males have been on the increase since

Table 2.16

Median and Mean Income Ratios for Black Females, White Females, and White Males, 1967–1984

Year	All Worker Median Income			"Corrected" Mean Income			Full-Time Median Income		
	Black Female/ White Male	White Female/ White Male	Black Female/ White Female	Black Female/ White Male	White Female/ White Male	Black Female/ White Female	Black Female/ White Male	White Female/ White Male	Black Female/ White Female
1967	.25	.28	.78	.25	.28	.89	.43	.58	.75
1968	.26	.33	.79	.25	.28	.91	.44	.58	.76
1969	.27	.32	.84	.26	.28	.91	.46	.58	.80
1970	.29	.32	.91	.27	.29	.95	.48	.59	.82
1971	.30	.34	.88	.28	.29	.96	.51	.58	.88
1972	.31	.33	.93	.28	.29	.98	.48	.57	.86
1973	.30	.33	.93	.27	.29	.93	.47	.56	.85
1974	.32	.36	.90	.29	.31	.94	.51	.56	.91
1975	.33	.37	.91	.31	.32	.96	.55	.57	.96
1976	.34	.36	.94	.32	.33	.96	.55	.59	.94
1977	.33	.38	.86	.32	.34	.94	.54	.58	.94
1978	.32	.36	.92	.33	.36	.91	.55	.59	.93
1979	.32	.35	.92	.33	.38	.88	.54	.59	.92
1980	.34	.37	.93	.34	.40	.86	.55	.59	.93
1981	.34	.39	.89	.34	.41	.84	.54	.60	.90
1982	.36	.40	.88	.36	.43	.83	.56	.62	.89
1983	.36	.42	.86	.37	.45	.82	.56	.63	.89
1984	.37	.42	.89	.38	.45	.84	.57	.63	.90

Source: See table 2-2.

Table 2.17
Black-White Unemployment Rates, Selected Years, 1948–1987

Year	Black Males	White Males	Black-White Ratio	Black Females	White Females	Black-White Ratio
1948[a]	5.8	3.4	1.71	6.1	3.4	1.79
1953[a]	4.8	2.5	1.92	4.1	3.1	1.32
1958[a]	13.8	6.1	2.26	10.8	6.2	1.74
1963[a]	20.5	4.7	2.23	11.2	5.8	1.93
1968[a]	5.6	2.6	2.15	8.3	4.3	1.93
1973[a]	7.7	3.8	2.03	10.6	5.3	2.00
1978[a]	11.0	4.6	2.39	13.0	6.2	2.10
1983[b]	20.3	8.8	2.31	18.6	7.9	2.35
1986[b]	14.8	6.0	2.47	14.2	6.1	2.33
1987[b]	12.7	5.4	2.35	13.2	5.2	2.54

[a]Blacks and other races
[b]Blacks alone
Sources of data: U.S. Dept. of Labor, *Manpower-Report to the President*, 1982, table A-28. Bureau of Labor Statistics, *Employment and Earnings Annual Averages*, January 1984 and January 1987.

1967, they also show how low those relative incomes were and still are. Among all workers, a black female had an income that was only 25% that of a white male in 1967. This proportion steadily increased to 37% in 1984. If the black female was a year-round, full-time worker, her proportion went from 43% in 1967 to 57% in 1984. However, as Table 2.4 indicates, only 32% to 35% of black females in the labor force were year-round, full-time workers during the 1967–1984 period, and so they do not fully represent the economic reality of black-female workers. "All Workers and All Persons" categories are more relevant for the consideration of relative black-female incomes, categories hardly illustrative of black economic progress.

It is inappropriate to leave the problem of black relative incomes without at least a passing glance at one of the proximate sources of the problem: black relative unemployment. The black unemployment rate is twice that of the white rate, as we see in Table 2.17. Whether the group observed is blacks alone or blacks and other races, the "twice the white rate" results are generally the same. These results have ominous new implications when coupled with the research Bluestone and Harrison (1986) have done on the types of jobs available to blacks in the new economy. They found that, between 1973 and 1979, 29% of net new employment among nonwhite males occurred in "low" wage jobs (those that paid $7,000 or less in 1984 dollars). Between 1979 and 1984, nearly 65% of all net new employment among nonwhite males was in such jobs. At the same time, between 1973 and 1979, 42% of net new employment of nonwhite males was in "high" wage jobs (those that paid $28,000 or more in 1984 dollars). Between 1973 and 1979, net new employment among nonwhite females was about 5% in low wage jobs and 10% in high wage jobs. Between 1979 and 1984, net new employment in low wage jobs had increased to 34%, while that in high wage jobs had fallen to 4%.

These trends suggest that the prospects for the black unemployed are increasingly limited and limiting. Commenting on the results of their study, Bluestone and Harrison (1986) noted that

> employment for minority men and women shows a renewed trend toward low wages. They added that this trend is an apparent reversal of the trend toward higher wage job opportunities for black men which was observed throughout much of the 1970s.

The racial gap is palpable, and yet it is not closing. To gain a richer understanding of the causes and the characteristics of the gap requires a careful discussion of two central phenomena: (1) the transition, over the course of the twentieth century, from capitalism to the managerial estate and (2) evolving patterns of class differentiation throughout American society and, specifically, within the native black population. Not only can the gap be best understood in such a context, but the context will illuminate the failure of a variety of strategies developed to close the gap, as well as the likely failure of certain "new" strategies being developed today.

The discussion undertaken here will also demonstrate the paradox that confronts native blacks in pursuit of equality in a society infused with and characterized by inequality. In a society with as dense a hierarchical structure as that of the United States, racial equality, much like gender equality, depends upon and demands a fundamental alteration of the structure itself. The analysis set out here should pose clearly the issues at stake for the survival and salvation of black America.

Finally, it should be noted at the outset that the use of the term "native blacks" is intended to emphasize that this report refers only to the historic black population in the United States, whose cultural and genealogical origins can be traced to the age of plantation slavery in North America. The essay does not analyze the conditions of more recent black immigrants—such as those from the Caribbean, West Africa, Ethiopia, or Uganda. This exclusion is not because of insensitivity to or lack of interest in their circumstances but because many aspects of their experiences are special to them and would require an entirely separate analysis.

The term "native blacks" is also used to avoid the ideologically popular term "minorities." The latter term has contributed to confounding the race question, which has stood at the heart of this nation's history since its founding, with a more recent panoply of "causes" that promote the interests of groups ranging from women to homosexuals to Vietnamese refugees. The idea of "minorities" deflects us from the main issue—the historical race question in the United States.

THE BLACK FAMILY IN THE MANAGERIAL AGE

The data already presented documents the lagging economic condition of the black family. But this condition is only one indicator of the scope of the crisis confronting America's native black population. To understand its full dimensions requires a substantive historical inquiry into the evolving scheme of social relations in contemporary America.

The two-parent family has long been the norm in American society. Among the various racial and ethnic subgroups in the United States, the native black population has experienced the most drastic decline in the representation of this traditional family structure. The fraction of black families headed by women has grown from 25% in the 1950s to 50% in recent years. It is among this growing group of black families headed by mothers that poverty strikes hardest and most harshly (Darity & Myers, 1984). Single-parent status also appears to be correlated with a variety of disadvantages for children that extend far beyond the direct limitations imposed by poverty status. For example, a child from a single-parent family has a greater probability of dropping out of school (Shaw, 1982; McLanahan, 1985). Although it is less well-documented, it has also been observed that juvenile delinquency and early pregnancies can be attributed to the experience of growing up in single-parent families.

The growth of female-headed families among blacks is symptomatic of conditions that lie well below the surface of statistics, well below such catchphrases as the "feminization of poverty." These phenomena are linked to the precarious status of black America as a whole in the current social milieu. The prevalence of black female–headed families is merely an indicator of an entire constellation of forces that negatively affect black Americans in our society.

The husband-wife family has always been relatively less the case among blacks than among other ethnic or racial groups in the United States. Slaveholders sought the breakup of family, tribe, and clan to individualize and subordinate the black population. Not only during the mature period of slavery, when importation of Africans had all but ceased, did the slaveholders seek, in some cases, to promote more conventional family life among their slaves. The slaveholders' motives, of course, were commercial; they sought some measure of family stability to ensure a stable labor supply. The commercial value of the chattel was the dominant consideration, leading the slaveholders to buy and sell slaves without consideration for relational ties. From the outset, then, black family life was assaulted in America; indeed, such assault was both fundamental to and a function of the system.

Emancipation led to feverish attempts to bring family members together. However, many former slaves remained unattached to any family unit because no family members could be found. The post-Reconstruction period was also characterized by an attempt on the part of the white aristocracy to regain control over black labor. The mechanism that restored many of the features of slave labor was the prison-lease system. The prison-lease system contributed to the ongoing breakup of the black family by simultaneously removing married black males from their families and preventing unmarried black males from forming new families.

Largely confined to the unskilled categories of the national labor market, black male labor was still viewed as valuable, at least in a reserve capacity, by industrialists in the early twentieth century. Industrialists turned to black workers as strikebreakers and as a pool of available cheaper wage contestants in the labor market. The movement of black workers from the South to the urban North, in response to such calls for cheaper labor, led to additional familial dislocations.[4]

Thus the forces undermining the black family from slavery times through the early part of the present century were consequences of attempts to utilize and control black labor—particularly black male labor—both within the slave system and the system that evolved after slavery. But from the 1930s onward the forces undermining the black family increasingly have been associated with a perceived lack of necessity of black labor—especially black male labor.

Whereas the conditions undermining the black family in the period prior to the 1930s were the character of capitalist development, largely within southern agriculture, since that time the conditions undermining the black family have been due to the development of a managerial society in the United States. Dominance by the business-financial elite in the United States gave way to dominance by the intellectuals and intelligentsia—the managerial class.[5]

The principle guiding capitalist development was the profitable command of labor, both labor in use and labor in reserve (unemployed); the principle guiding managerial development has been the scientific discharge of labor from the workplace, particularly manual labor. This pattern of discharge has meant the progressive marginalization of black males, long excluded from extensive participation in nonmanual and so-called knowledge occupations. Now large numbers of black males are faced with the elimination of the occupational categories for which they qualify. As the black male is moved further and further out to the margins of America's economy and society, this necessarily has repercussions for the black family.

The microelectronic-cum-robotics revolution has laid the groundwork for the elimination of a whole range of occupations, particularly manufacturing, without replacing those positions with new work. This is not a uniquely American phenomenon; it is occurring worldwide. A decade ago in a special report prepared for the president of France, Nora and Minc (1978) commented, "Given the increasing automation of industry, most industrial managers state that growth in the coming years will be accomplished without increases in manpower—in fact, that manpower will decrease slightly, unless demand rises at an unusual rate" (pp. 38–39). In a 1980 study prepared for the International Labour Office, Juan Rada concluded that "a transition is taking place from a society with unemployment to one that no longer needs its full potential labour force to produce the necessary goods and services under current conditions of work" (p. 105). In a similar vein, Ernest Mandel (1980) observed in his 1978 Marshall Lectures at Cambridge, "new radical substitution of machines for men (in fact, the new wave of automation could be characterized as 'robotism') would almost unavoidably imply massive reduction in total productive employment" (p. 108). Mandel specifically referred to studies in West Germany and Japan that revealed prospects for the massive elimination of industrial workers' jobs in both countries via robotics. In West Germany 4.3 workers per robot was the estimated reduction; in Japan estimates indicated that one-third of the existing industrial work force in 1978 could be eliminated by 1988, and 90% within 20 to 30 years, while maintaining 1978 levels of output.

In the United States, since late 1982 (as estimated by the Federal Reserve Board's index), manufacturing output has grown almost 30%, whereas employment in manufacturing grew only 6%. In 1986 output in manufacturing grew 1%, while the absolute number of jobs fell by 200,000. In the automobile industry the 1986 figures are even more striking. Wharton Econometrics estimates that output per hour has risen 5.6% while man-hours have fallen 3.2% (Clark, 1986, p. 1). A study of these structural changes in the U.S. economy undertaken by Leontief and Duchin (1986) leads them to conclude that the intensive use of automation will make it possible to achieve over the next 20 years significant economies in labor relative to the production of the same bills of goods with the technologies currently in use. And who is to say what the consequences of future technologies will be?

Charles Silberman (1966) issued an early challenge to this scenario in the 1960s. He suggested that despite his own expectation that eventually "we shall have the technical capability to substitute machines for men in most of the functions men now perform . . . the decision to automate would still be an investment decision—not a scientific decision" (p. 2). In effect he said that human labor can compete with machines by offering to work for lower wages: "In the last analysis, men will not be replaced by machines because widespread substitution of machines for men would tend to reduce the price of the latter and increase the price of the former" (p. 22). This appears to be precisely the type of leverage exercised recently by Weyerhauser Corporation when it "weathered a six-week strike to force workers to accept wage cuts averaging 20%" (Clark, 1986, p. 20). Silberman's answer to those who contend that workers will be displaced relatively, and perhaps absolutely, by technical change is to point out that laborers can offer to work for less. Unless, however, the productivity gains lead to concomitant reductions in output prices, workers will be accepting real reductions in their standard of living.

What underlies Silberman's response is the belief that technical change will continue to be profit motivated. However, as capitalism winds down and the managerial era supplants it, "scientific decisions" are replacing "investment decisions." In such an environment, there will be no barrier to the replacement of labor with machinery. Devendra Garg (1986) estimates that the spread of automation throughout U.S. industry could have an effect on almost half of the work force; automation is unlikely to create as many jobs as it destroys because robots can build other robots.

Capitalist development originated the process of continuous, albeit unsteady, reductions in labor time. This reduction generated a reserve of labor, a reserve that is disproportionately black in the United States. This reserve—not employed but not unemployable—serves at least two functions: it provides employers with a ready pool of workers to draw upon during the periods of rapid industrial expansion, and it serves as a restraint on the demands of employed workers (Marx, 1977).

In contrast, for the managerial class this reserve of labor is without function. As the momentum of technical change renders labor superfluous, from a managerial perspective the "excess" population carried over from capitalist to postcapitalist society is genuinely unnecessary (Darity, 1983). In a remarkably prescient study, Donald Michael (1962) identified a number of procedures to cope with a population that is not needed to perform work: (1) put people into public works projects, (2) relocate people to regions or nations where automation is not yet so extensive, (3) reduce the birth rate, and (4) lower the retirement age. Aside from procedure number 3, Michael saw problems arising from each of these steps. He did not articulate the two gruesome alternatives of incarceration and extermination, but he was explicitly aware that when cybernation takes hold there will indeed be a population deemed extraneous and thus subject to containment measures.

The position of the black male—and the black population in general—must be understood in the context of these broader trends and developments. Black males are overwhelmingly members of the working class, and in particular are represented in the inactive or surplus portion of the working class. Among their numbers are a large percentage of persons rarely employed, deeply entrenched in poverty, most likely to be imprisoned, most likely to be the military's foot soldiers, and least likely to have a sense of optimism about the opportunities offered by American society. This segment of the black working class is referred to by sociologists as the black "underclass" (Wilson, 1980). Moreover, there is no evident place for them in the managerial age, as race and class harden into caste under circumstances where intergenerational social mobility becomes ever more elusive.

INTRARACIAL INEQUALITY IN THE MANAGERIAL AGE

The broad lines of class division that exist in America as a whole—between capital, labor, and the managerial class—are replicated in native black America. The black middle class consists of an intellectual-professional element as well as a business element. The latter element is of far less importance than the former, but the two combined comprise "the black elite."

The black business element is notorious for the relative modesty of its enterprises, as well as for the insignificance of its output in the U.S. economy as a whole. Romantic notions of "black capitalism" notwithstanding, the black businessperson has never been a serious force, has never produced substantial economic progress in black America. When E. Franklin Frazier (1957) wrote his classic study of the black middle class, he referred accurately to "the myths of Negro business." Those myths are still promulgated by some who fantasize about a black American entrepreneurial heyday, despite the marginal position of black business and the waning of the business age.[6] The black businessperson's wealth may be large relative to other blacks, but it is small relative to the wealth of white owners and directors of the nation's major corporations.

The second major element of the black elite is the intellectual-professional group—doctors, lawyers, ministers, educators, social workers, etc. This is the managerial stratum of the black community. Its functional role has largely been the supervision and social management of the black working class.[7] It is this class that is the source of the ideological stance attributed to black America in general by the media, deeply attached to the idea of achieving racial equality. And it is useful to note, as Frazier (1957, p. 85) observed, that "from the beginning the Negro intelligentsia, or what Du Bois called the 'Talented Tenth,' was created by philanthropic foundations supported by northern industrialists."[8]

There is some ambiguity concerning the size of the black middle class. Those who identify it strictly in economic terms—for example, by characterizing as middle class all families of four with $20,000 or more in income in 1980 dollars—find that about 20% of the black population is now middle class (McGhee, 1982). But the approach of this report is to identify class position by social function rather than merely by income. Educational credentials separate the black managerial class from the black working class in the same manner that educational credentials separate the managerial class in general from the masses.

Based upon this approach the black middle class may be only 7 to 10% of the black population. The precise number is not what really matters. What counts is that the black managerial class—despite substantial growth in the 1960s—is small in proportion to the overall black population, and especially small when compared with representation in the same class by the nonblack majority or by other ethnic groups in the United States.[9]

There is sharp divergence between the lifestyles, attitudes, perceptions, and material well-being of the members of the black managerial class and the black underclass. It is as if they are planets spinning on opposite sides of the sun. But at the same time that their contrasting experiences push these two elements of the black community further and further apart, the structure of the post–New Deal social programs joins them at the hip, Siamese twins of welfare.

The gap between the black managerial class and the black underclass has statistical manifestations nearly as pronounced as the gap between blacks as a whole and the nonblack majority. The depths of the difference crystallize in the following observations:

1. The black underclass is the site of the most fragile family circumstances. By 1981, 46%—almost half—of the approximately 6.4 million black families in the United States were headed by women (U.S. Bureau

Table 2.18
Welfare Recipients, by Length of Welfare Receipt, 1969–1978

Number of Years of Welfare Receipt	Black	Total Population
1	14.9[a]	31.3
2-5	39.0	42.9
6-9	30.9	17.9
10	15.2	7.9

[a]14.9% of black persons who received welfare incomes at any time between 1969 and 1978 received it for only year.
Source of data: A Preliminary Empirical Examination of the Dynamics of Welfare Use (p. 131), by R.D. Coe, in *Analysis of the First Twelve Years of the Panel Study of Income Dynamics*, Vol. 9 of *Five Thousand American Families–Patterns of Economic Progress*, 1974-, University of Michigan: Survey Research Center, Institute for Social Research.

Table 2.19
Distribution of Population, by Number of Years of Welfare Receipt, 1969–1979

	Welfare[a] Receipt			Welfare Amounted to ≥50% of Income		
Number of Years	Black	White	Black as a Percent of Total	Black	White	Black as a Percent of Total
0	51.0[b]	83.9	6.0[c]	66.1	91.3	8.3
1	7.9	4.9	13.7	6.6	1.9	40.6
2-5	20.8	6.6	26.3	14.3	4.1	41.4
6-9	14.2	3.2	49.6	9.8	2.0	56.9
10	6.2	1.4	54.8	3.2	0.7	55.3
1-10	49.0	16.1		33.9	8.7	

[a]AFDC,SSI, general assistance payments, old age assistance, aid to the disabled, and food stamps.
[b]51% of the black population did not receive income from welfare in any year between 1969 and 1978.
[c]6% of the families who did not receive income from welfare in any year between 1969 and 1978 were black.
Source: See Table 2-18, pp. 142, 163-164.

of Census, 1983b, p. 102). These families with absent fathers form the heart of the black underclass. In 1981, 68% of such families with children under 18 years of age received incomes below the poverty line (U.S. Bureau of Census, 1983a, p. 8). The experiences of these women heading families contrast sharply with those of the black professional women who have children late in life or have none at all. But both groups face declining prospects for black male mates—black poor women because of the low relative numbers of marriageable black men and black professional women because of the low relative numbers of comparably educated black men. To point up this latter discrepancy, black women are now enrolling at major universities at two times the rate of black men.

2. Court decisions related to family life have progressively pushed female-headed families toward reliance on social transfer programs as a means of support.[10] Today the welfare crisis can be identified justifiably with the crisis in black family life. Economist Richard Coe (1982), using longitudinal data from the University of Michigan's Panel Study of Income Dynamics, found that more than half of the recipients of welfare for eight or more years between 1969 and 1978 were black. In addition, Coe found that nearly 60% of all black females who were heads of households or wives in 1970 received welfare at some point between 1969 and 1978. Among these women, 40% received welfare for five years or more, and 30% received welfare for eight years or more. (Also see Tables 2.18 and 2.19.)

3. In a broader sense, the black underclass is heavily dependent on federal transfer programs as a source of income. A 1983 report in *The Washington Post* revealed

> One out of every four blacks in America is now enrolled in Medicaid, the largest federal welfare program. One in four gets food stamps, the second largest program. One out of every five receives aid to families with dependent children (AFDC), the largest welfare program that pays cash. One of every seven lives in federally subsidized housing. (Coleman, p. A1)

It is also pertinent to note here that while 2% of white male–headed families, 6% of black male–headed families, and 15% of white female–headed families received public assistance and welfare income in 1981, 40% of black female–headed families received those categories of income (see Table 2.20). The mean dollar amount from these types of income received by black female–headed families came to more than $3,100 during the same year.

It is easy to document black underclass dependence on the social programs inaugurated in the 1930s and greatly expanded in the 1960s. It is also easy to document, but less widely recognized, that the black managerial class is heavily dependent on these same programs from the other side of the fence: the earnings of the black managerial class are received in large measure from public sector positions that involve administration of the social programs. The recent growth and "progress" of the black managerial class can be traced directly to the expansion of social welfare programs under the rubric of the Great Society. The following lengthy observation from Brown and Erie (1981) is especially pertinent:

Table 2.20

Families, by Race and Gender, of HEA with Income from Public Assistance and Supplemental Security Income, 1975–1983 (Percentage of Distribution)

Year	Public Assistance & Supplemental Security Income				Public Assist & Welfare Income				Supplemental Security Income			
	Female		Male		Female		Male		Female		Male	
	Black	White	Black	White	Black	White	Black	White	Black	White	Black	White
1983	43.2[a]	17.3	10.1	3.1	37.4	13.7	5.4	1.7	9.0	4.3	5.8	1.5
1982	42.2	18.2	10.4	2.0	37.2	14.6	6.1	1.7	8.0	4.5	5.0	1.4
1981	46.6	18.9	11.2	3.1	39.6	15.5	6.4	1.7	10.2	4.4	5.8	1.5
1980	46.2	19.4	12.1	3.2	38.2	15.9	7.4	1.9	12.0	4.9	5.7	1.5
1979	49.2	19.1	11.6	3.0	41.3	15.3	7.0	1.7	12.0	4.9	5.8	1.5
1978	55.0	24.4	13.0	3.2	46.5	19.8	7.8	1.8	11.5	6.0	6.2	1.6
1977	53.6	23.9	13.0	3.4	46.5	19.6	7.3	1.9	10.3	5.6	7.0	1.7
1976	55.0	24.9	12.3	3.4	48.6	20.3	7.5	1.9	11.0	5.9	6.0	1.7
1975	53.7	25.9	11.9	3.4	47.1	21.2	7.4	1.9	11.2	5.8	6.9	1.8

[a]In 1983, 43.2% of black families with female heads received income from public assistance or supplemental security income at some time during that year.

Source: U.S. Bureau of Census, *Current Population Reports, Consumer Income*, No. 80, pp. 86, 88; No. 85, pp. 96, 98; No. 90, pp. 105, 107; No. 97, pp. 103, 105; No. 105, p. 126; No. 114, p. 127; No. 118, p. 119; No. 123, p. 148; No. 129, p. 138; No. 132, p. 116; No. 137, p. 104; No. 142, p. 104; No. 146, p. 105.

expanding public social welfare employment has served as a major port of entry for the new black middle class . . . 55% of the 1960–76 increase in black professional, managerial, and technical employment (PATs) occurred in the public sector, compared with 34% for whites. Social welfare programs accounted for nearly one-half of the black middle-class increase, compared with one-quarter for whites. As of 1976, 45% of all black professionals, administrators, and technicians were in public social welfare programs, compared with 19% of comparably situated whites. At the federal level, 42% of all black PATs were in DHEW, HUD, Labor, CSA, or the VA compared with 18% of whites. At the state and local level, 68% of all black PATs employed outside education (compared with 39% of whites) were in social welfare agencies. It is true that at least since the New Deal black professionals and administrators have been more likely to be employed in the public sector than whites. In this regard developments in the 1960s represent merely the extension of an historical trend. But if the attractiveness of public employment among the black middle class has not changed, something else has. Prior to 1960 black professionals and administrators were concentrated in education and, at the federal level, in the post office. The significant shift in the 1960s is that middle class blacks moved into noneducational social welfare agencies at the state and local level. Moreover, prior to 1960 the black middle class was relatively small. Between 1960 and 1976, the size of the black middle class roughly tripled. (pp. 308–309)

Herein lies the source of Richard Freeman's "dramatic progress" for blacks. The expansion of means-tested income maintenance programs for the poor under the aegis of the Great Society constituted an income maintenance program for the black managerial class as well. Tables 2.21 and 2.22 make clear the connection between growth in the black professional stratum and social welfare employment. As Brown and Erie (1981) conclude: "The principal economic legacy of the Great Society for the black community . . . has been the creation of a large-scale social welfare economy of publicly funded middle-income service providers and low-income service and cash transfer receipts" (p. 311). Here we find precisely how these two classes within black America are joined, while their daily lives gravitate in opposing directions.

The Great Society can thus be seen as a set of policy initiatives which, much like the New Deal, benefitted the managerial class broadly. The specific impact on the black middle class was quite dramatic and points to a host of disturbing implications, the first of which concerns the black middle class's dream of racial equality. To the extent that racial inequality amounts to the black middle class being too small in number relative to the nonblack majority middle class, the obvious prescription is to expand further the black middle class. But if the expansion is conducted on the

Table 2.21[a]
Social Welfare Employment Gains, by Gender and Race, 1960–1980

	Nonagricultural Civilian Employment (in thousands)[b]							
	Females				Males			
	White		Black		White		Black	
Year	%	(N)	%	(N)	%	(N)	%	(N)
1960								
Social Welfare[c]	23.5%		20.0%		5.9%		8.5%	
Other	76.5		80.0		94.1		91.5	
Total	100.0	(16269)	100.0	(2119)	100.0	(30706)	100.0	(2851)
1969								
Social Welfare	26.7		29.3		8.6		10.9	
Other	73.3		70.7		91.4		89.1	
Total	100.0	(23363)	100.0	(3122)	100.0	(37326)	100.0	(3842)
1973								
Social Welfare	29.1		34.8		9.2		12.5	
Other	70.9		65.2		90.8		87.5	
Total	100.0	(26202)	100.0	(3147)	100.0	(40012)	100.0	(4072)
1977								
Social Welfare	30.2		35.8		10.4		11.9	
Other	69.8		64.2		89.6		88.1	
Total	100.0	(29651)	100.0	(3674)	100.0	(41213)	100.0	(3994)
1980								
Social Welfare	30.2		39.0		10.6		13.4	
Other	69.8		61.0		89.4		86.6	
Total	100.0	(33428)	100.0	(4168)	100.0	(43362)	100.0	(4224)
Social Welfare Share of Employment Increase								
1960-1980	36.5%		58.6%		22.0%		23.6%	
1960-1969	34.3		49.1		21.2		18.0	
1969-1973	48.9		92.9		17.0		38.7	
1973-1977	38.6		49.0		50.4		(43.6)[d]	
1977-1980	30.2		37.0		14.4		39.6	

[a]Table provided by M.K. Brown.
[b]As reported in March survey week.
[c]Includes medical, hospital, education, welfare, and religious employment.
[d]Social welfare share of employment decrease for black males, 1973-1977.
Sources of data: U.S. Bureau of the Census, *Public Use Sample*, 1960; U.S. Bureau of the Census, *Current Population Survey*, 1969, 1973, 1977, and 1980, March Supplement. Data tapes supplied by the Inter-University Consortium for Political Research, University of Michigan.

Table 2.22
Professional, Administrative, and Technical Employment Gains, by Gender and Race, 1960–1980[b]

	Nonagricultural Civilian Employment (in thousands)[b]							
	Females				Males			
	White		Black		White		Black	
Year	%	(N)	%	(N)	%	(N)	%	(N)
1960								
Social Welfare[c]								
Other	24.3		9.7		81.9		40.6	
Total	100.0	(2911)	100.0	(185)	100.0	(6436)	100.0	(138)
1973								
Social Welfare	69.6		81.8		22.3		44.9	
Other	30.4		18.2		77.7		55.1	
Total	100.0	(5220)	100.0	(488)	100.0	(11024)	100.0	(401)
1977								
Social Welfare	65.8		80.8		23.8		38.6	
Other	34.2		19.2		76.2		61.4	
Total	100.0	(6460)	100.0	(614)	100.0	(12271)	100.0	(479)
1980								
Social Welfare	61.0		77.7		22.8		35.9	
Other	39.0		22.3		77.2		64.1	
Total	100.0	(8281)	100.0	(670)	100.0	(13518)	100.0	(530)
Social Welfare Share of PAT Employment Increase								
1960-1980	53.0%		72.8%		27.1%		27.6%	
1960-1973	61.9		76.6		28.2		37.3	
1973-1977	49.8		77.0		37.0		6.4	
1977-1980	43.9		44.6		13.0		9.8	

[a]Table provided by M.K. Brown.
[b]As reported in March survey week.
[c]Includes medical, hospital, education, welfare, and religious employment.
Sources: See table 2-2.

basis of increasing social welfare employment there must be clients to be served. Therefore, the black middle class, as constituted at present, needs a black underclass to justify its own occupational status. Too much racial equality undermines the service providers' own reason for being. On the other hand, the alternative reform offered by the business interests—abolition of the welfare state—threatens to leave only the "private charities" to assist the poor, while other options offered by social managers, for example, Senator Moynihan's recent enthusiasm for workfare arrangements, are unremittingly punitive in character.

The second related implication of the policies of the Great Society concerns the tendency of the black managerial class—like the managerial class broadly—to support programmatic initiatives alleged to uplift all blacks when, in fact, the managers are the main beneficiaries. If the entire nexus of policies adopted in the 1960s are taken as a whole, not one can be found to have a net positive impact on the condition of the black underclass. For instance, Charles Brown (1982) has found that if affirmative action has had an effect on behalf of blacks, the effect appears to be concentrated among blacks "at the upper end of the skill distribution" (p. 60). Balancing and busing to achieve school desegregation left unaddressed the more fundamental issue of quality education. Antidiscrimination laws for housing were largely irrelevant for those financially unable to buy a new home. Manpower training programs prepared participants for nonexistent or marginal jobs. As pointed out above, the general expansion of transfer programs has reinforced the dependent status of the black underclass—dependent on federal largesse—and it has also nurtured the growth of the black managerial class. This is not to say that the Civil Rights Act of 1964 should not have been passed. It is to say that it did not and could not address the fundamental sources of racial inequality.

The peculiar vulnerability of the black middle class now becomes clear in the context of the greater class war. The Reagan administration's budget cutbacks—especially those aimed at social welfare programs—amounted to a direct assault on the occupations obtained by members of the black elite during the recent period of "dramatic progress." With the Reagan retrenchment well underway the consequences were already being felt. As *The Washington Post* reported in 1983:

> At the federal level, blacks and members of other minority groups accounted for one of every three persons laid off or downgraded as a result of Reagan retrenchment. Black administrators were laid off at a rate three times that of white administrators and nearly three and one-half times that of lower-level black employees. (Coleman, p. A18)

Still, the impact has not yet been as devastating as one might have expected because Congress stabilized expenditures and state and local governments took on a greater role in maintaining social welfare programs. Nevertheless, the peculiar vulnerability of the black middle class has been clearly exposed.

It is no surprise, then, that the black middle class stood in opposition to the Reagan agenda. Their tendency, however, was to revert to endorsement of the social programs that gave them their moment in the sun, despite those programs' failure to uplift the black masses. The reversion carries some still deeper dangers.

Corporate capital's mission, which found its strategic expression in Reagan policies, is to curb the pretensions of the managerial class—to make some members of that class efficient functionaries on behalf of business and to cast others back into the working class where they may be made over into productive laborers.

On the other hand, the managerial class, particularly the broader non-black element, will find less and less reason to retain the excess population. Its rational view of production—unmotivated by the pursuit of profit—leads it to see no compelling reason to maintain a reserve of unemployed workers. Over the long term it will move to eliminate superfluous layers of the working class. Since those layers most likely to be deemed superfluous are disproportionately black (as Wilhelm anticipated in *Who Needs the Negro?*), these are grim times indeed for the black underclass. Moreover, as the black underclass is reduced, the segment of the black population that "ministers" to the underclass—the black managerial class—also will have no social function. What purpose is there for service providers if there are no service recipients?

The superfluity of the black underclass is reinforced by technological developments (microelectronics-cum-robotics) that reduce the social necessity for all labor. It is aggravated further by the new immigrants who stand as replacements—for the new immigrants are less jaded, less rebellious, and less expensive workers.

In the short term the broad managerial class may promise *and deliver* a renewed expansion of social programs to garner the political support of both the black managerial class and the black underclass. But the longer term tendency is for the broad managerial class to prune away superfluous elements. Once power is consolidated, the voting support of black Americans will no longer be required, and the cost of maintenance of the disruptive and nonaccommodative black poor will come to be viewed as too expensive. Steps will be taken to prune away the black underclass, and, concomitantly, the black social managers as well.

While capitalist society sought to make every black a laborer, managerial society calls into question the utility of blacks. Managerial society is in the process of declaring "the Negro" obsolete. Capitalist society threatened the class status of the black elite, but the managerial revolution threatens the very existence of black America as a cultural entity.

This threat is implicit in the silence of the new managerial strategy on the race question. The New Industrial Policy (NIP), the economic prong of the "new" ideas being advanced by the managerial class, amounts to nothing more than a "trickle down" argument concerning benefits for black America.[11] Only now the "trickle down" benefits would emanate from a recovery engineered through national planning rather than a recovery engineered, as Reaganomics would have had it, through the "natural" workings of the "free" market. On the rare occasions when proponents of NIP advance specific solutions to improve the black condition, they merely echo the New Deal–Civil Rights–Great Society programs.

Suffice it to say, *neither* path offers an authentic beacon of hope for the black underclass, or for the black population at large. Ralph Bunche (1936), when confronted with a similar unsatisfactory fork in the road in the 1930s, reached a similar conclusion:

> For the Negro population, the New Deal means the same thing, but more of it. Striking at no fundamental social conditions, the New Deal at best can only fix the disadvantages, the differentials, the discriminations under which the Negro population has labored all along. . . .
>
> . . . New Deal planning only serves to crystallize those abuses and oppressions which the exploited Negro citizenry of America have long suffered under laissez-faire capitalism, and for the same reasons as in the past. (p. 65)

The choice now appears to be between a refurbished laissez-faire capitalism and a New Deal. Neither alternative holds much promise for closing the gap for black America. Both alternatives contain threats to the survival and salvation of native black America.

DISCRIMINATION IN THE MANAGERIAL AGE

As the necessity for labor in the aggregate—particularly unskilled or low-skilled labor—continues to decline, the struggle to secure the remaining places on the occupational ladder will intensify. Racial and ethnic conflict will continue apace as groups seek to secure niches in the hierarchy of managerial society. In such an environment racial discrimination will continue, transmuted along new and more subtle lines by antidiscrimination legislation and litigation.

The dimensions of discrimination by race are vast, ranging from the exclusion of black youths from college preparatory tracks, to channelling black youths away from hard sciences, to outright exclusion from occupations. Particularly striking is the changing character of exclusion following the introduction of federal antidiscrimination measures. These measures did not address the power base of other ethnic contestants for occupational turf or the incentives that exist for turf preservation. Only the decorative exteriors of discrimination were addressed, not the brick and mortar. The laws have merely produced new procedures to perpetuate exclusion. In their recent study on the structure of earnings, Taylor, Gwartney-Gibbs, and Farley (1986) find no sector of the U.S. economy that does not display significant discriminatory earnings differentials in the aftermath of antidiscrimination legislation.

In many different occupations, including jobs in the public sector such as in police and fire departments, the ascent of white workers up the seniority ladder was made easier because nonwhites were systematically excluded from competition for these jobs. Various union seniority systems were established at a time when racial minorities were barred from employment and union membership. Obviously blacks as a group, not just as individuals, constituted a class of victims who could not develop seniority status. A seniority system launched under these conditions inevitably becomes the institutionalized mechanism whereby whites as a group are granted racial privilege.[12]

But in the unfolding managerial age it is necessary to look out for mechanisms and sites of exclusion other than those traditionally associated with union activity. In the age of science and technology it is the academy that assigns credibility, credentials, and the imprimatur of authority. How do native blacks fare in obtaining access to quality institutions of higher education?

One could just as well ask how blacks fare in obtaining quality educational experiences at all levels. The example of the city of Chicago is revealing. Nearly one-half of the students from Chicago's public schools do not finish high school, and this proportion is overwhelmingly black.[13] Of course without a high school diploma a student is not even eligible for college admission.

The University of Illinois at Chicago (UIC), which enrolls primarily a regional undergraduate student body, has undergone an overall enrollment decline since 1979. But the decline in black student enrollment has been 40%, considerably more significant than the overall drop. Moreover, among black students actually matriculating, the attrition rate is astonishing. Whereas 30.4% of white students entering UIC in the fall of 1981 had graduated by 1987, only 7.4% of the black students had. For the class entering in 1982, while 25% of the white students had graduated by 1987, only 4.4% of the black students had done so.[14]

The UIC case may be somewhat extreme, but it symptomatic of a national trend. At a major southern university, the University of North Carolina at Chapel Hill, black undergraduates experience academic suspension rates three times as high as those of white students.[15] The limited capacity of native blacks to gain from the academy and to influence the academy also is demonstrated by the drop in black enrollment in graduate schools. After peaking in the 1970s, the percentage of black graduate students has fallen from 5.1% in 1976 to 4.2% in 1982. Blacks remain a stable 4.6% of the professional school population. Sociologist Gail Thomas has offered the following explanations:

- The low quality of elementary and secondary schools in predominantly black areas channels black youths away from access to and interest in higher education.
- Guidance counselors fail to encourage black youths to pursue advanced degrees.
- The screening methods used to select students, given the traditionally poor performance of blacks on the SAT and the GRE, work against blacks whose performance on such tests is hampered by test bias and the lack of early and adequate exposure to standardized tests.

Consistent with the broader themes of this report Thomas warns, "Blacks are at a dangerous point in terms of becoming disempowered as a result of what I see as a disturbing trend in higher education" (Associated Press, 1987, p. 17A).[16]

Blacks also are disappearing from the ranks of PhD holders. Fields such as engineering, the physical sciences, and mathematics now consistently have less than 2% black representation among their doctorates. Between 1977 and 1987 the number of doctorates awarded to black American males declined 54%, from 684 to 317, lower than the absolute number awarded to Asian-American men in the same year.[17] The cumulative effect of negligible black representation in these fields is a complete dearth of black influence in the dissemination of knowledge, credentials, status, and authority. It reinforces the marginal status of the native black population in the era of science and technology.

Again with respect to the specific Chicago case, across all Chicago area universities less than 3% of the faculties are black. Blacks are disproportionately untenured. It has been suggested that the lower tenure ratios for blacks are due to age (blacks on average are younger PhD recipients) and to the greater difficulty in obtaining tenure today. But the gap would persist even if the age distribution was the same, and even if tenure criteria had not stiffened, because a greater percentage of blacks are on nontenure-track appointments. For example, at UIC 32.7% of black and Hispanic faculty are not on tenure track compared with 17% of whites (Reis, 1987).

Further difficulties involve the concentration of black academics in history, sociology, and Afro-American studies. Moreover, less credibility is accorded research by black scholars doing racial research than is accorded white scholars. Black administrators, to a disproportionate degree, are not faculty members, making them more vulnerable to job loss if they take strong stands and less able to protect black faculty members faced with tenure denial. The fewer the blacks, the more prestigious the university. For example, in Chicago, while 14.9% of the faculty at Northeastern Illinois is black, only 2.6% of the faculty at Northwestern University is black (Reis, 1987).

The current trends seem locked in place, for the near term at least. Nationally in 1980–81 blacks received only 3.3% of undergraduate engineering degrees and a mere 1.6% of master's degrees. Less than 1% of engineering PhDs were blacks. In 1980–81 blacks received 5.2% of the undergraduate degrees in biological sciences, largely from predominantly black schools, but only 2.9% of the master's degrees, and 1.7% of the PhDs; blacks received 4% of the BAs in the physical sciences (also largely from black schools), 2% of the master's degrees, and 1% of the doctorates; and in mathematics, blacks received 5.3% the BAs (again largely from black schools), 2.6% of the master's degrees, and only 1.2% of PhDs (Reis, 1987).

The American Council on Education estimates that American colleges and universities have 18,827 full-time black faculty—4% of the total, a drop from 19,674 in 1977. Blacks constitute only 2.3% of the faculty at predominantly white institutions; 8,200 black educators are concentrated at 100 predominantly black college campuses—institutions with less resources, less prestige, and less influence than their white counterparts (Duvall, 1987).

The phenomenon of black exclusion from the academy is of special significance in the managerial age. It indicates how widely the social dimensions of discriminatory practices stretch. The relative absence of blacks from the academy begins with the differential in opportunities afforded by family resources and the differential in the quality of schooling in the early years; it continues with the deflecting of black college students from fields with greater technical requirements; and it concludes with the ghettoization of the residual of black academics in a handful of less respected subfields of research. Ultimately, blacks have negligible influence on the standards and procedures that govern access to the academy.

Antidiscrimination laws have not and cannot exercise much effect on these circumstances. Competition between ethnic and racial cliques produces the perpetuation of discrimination rather than its elimination. We are witnessing the historical outcome for the group that was always viewed by other (European) contesting groups as unworthy of entry into the ethnic social compromise over the allocation of occupational turf. Black workers consistently would be relegated to less skilled jobs or denied jobs altogether. Matters only become worse when the range of available well-paid, blue-collar occupations narrows with structural change in the U.S. economy; after all, the discriminatory nature of the educational process inherently limits opportunities available to blacks.

CONCLUSIONS

Race continues to matter. Discrimination persists, although its forms have altered. The intrinsic nature of American society is geared toward ethnic/racial competition, the struggle to carve out social turf for one's own group. The conflict works itself out in classic forms of American tribalism.

Blacks enter the turf wars with various disadvantages. Per capita income and (especially) wealth are comparatively low. Professional-level blacks frequently have supervisory or quasi-supervisory positions in social welfare administration, so that there is no significant basis for blacks to act independently of public sector "helping" positions. The relative deterioration of schooling, family life, health conditions, and so on, all reinforce the disadvantages in racial/ethnic competition. And blacks have already lost many previous rounds of turf wars, since other contesting groups could all agree not to compromise with blacks. Class cleavages among blacks compound the difficulties in becoming successful competitors.

Familial and schooling crises are not uniquely black problems. These same symptoms of deterioration now appear among other groups. But among blacks these conditions are more acute and more visible, both anecdotally and statistically. And they layer on top of the inferior black position in America's ethnic/racial struggles.

If blacks are to be a healthy and contributing presence in the United States, the options are straightforward. Either the compromise must finally be struck, formally or informally, and native blacks granted an appropriate set of positions in managerial society's social structure, or a struggle must be waged against the structure itself. The former route means blacks must opt fully for a representative share of real (rather than merely racial) equality. The latter route means a far more radical course of action and would require calling into question the values that produced success in our competitive and hierarchical society.

I have touched upon the most troubling prospect of all: that a continued black presence is by no means assured. For in the transition from capitalism to managerialism those relegated to the surplus population will find their very existence threatened. In fact, to the extent that *blacks* are viewed as the social problem, and hence objects of social management, rather than the *system* being viewed as the social problem, the danger should be clear. What is happening in black America today merely foreshadows the full force inherent in the rise of the managerial estate. Not only will the question "Who needs the Negro?" be voiced with greater frequency, but the question: "Who *is* needed and who is *not*?" will be applied broadly across the entire population. The answers are likely to be as chilling as the question.

NOTES

1. See, e.g., *Race Differences in Earnings: A Survey and New Evidence*, by J. P. Smith and F. Welch, published in March 1978, by the Rand Corporation of Santa Monica, CA; and *Closing the Gap: Forty Years of Economic Progress for Blacks*, by the same authors, published in February 1986, by the Rand Corporation. Smith and Welch contend that black "gains" are due to improvements in the quality and quantity of black education and blacks' transition from southern, mainly agricultural, labor to northern industrial wage labor. In another article by Smith and Welch, entitled Black Economic Progress After Myrdal, published in the *Journal of Economic Literature, 27*, in June 1989, they acknowledge that South-to-North migration no longer serves as a vehicle for black economic gain.

2. For a compact and thorough critique of the optimistic reading, see J. P. Cotton's article Some Observations of Closing the Gap, published in the *Trotter Institute Review, 1* (1), Winter 1987, by the William Monroe Trotter Institute, University of Massachusetts at Boston, pages 13–16; and Cotton's article Opening the Gap: The Decline in Black Economic Indicators in the 1980s, published in *Social Science Quarterly, 70* (4), 803, December 1989.

3. In an excellent recent survey of these issues, J. J. Heckman has complained that the Darity-Myers assumption that nonworkers make zero earnings is "extreme." Still, as the econometrician who has done the basic research on selection bias problems, he long has argued that the labor force dropout phenomenon has biased the data on black-white differences toward an optimistic reading. He seems to place more credence in C. Brown's finding that two-thirds of the measured black gain for males is due to underaccounting for poor blacks. See J. J. Heckman's article The Impact of Government on the Economic Status of Black Americans in *The Question of Discrimination*, edited by S. Shulman

and W. Darity, Jr., published in 1989, by Wesleyan University Press, Middletown, CT.

4. For the classic analysis, see E. F. Frazier's *The Negro Family in the United States*, published in 1939 by the University of Chicago Press.

5. See W. Darity, Jr.'s, article The Managerial Class and Industrial Policy, published in *Industrial Relations*, *25* (2), Spring 1986, pages 212–27; and also Darity's article The Managerial Class and Surplus Population, published in *Society*, *21* (1), November-December 1983, pages 54–62. For an earlier classic discussion of the managerial class that differs from Darity's, see T. Kemp's article The Intelligentsia and Modern Capitalism, published in *Science and Society*, *26* (3), Summer 1962, pages 309–325.

6. It is anecdotal, but telling nonetheless, that typically no black-owned business on the *Black Enterprise* top 100 list comes close to making the Fortune 500 list.

7. In his book *Black Bourgeoisie*, published in 1957 by The Free Press, Glencoe, IL, E. F. Frazier made the following comment during the era of enforced segregation:

> Since the black bourgeoisie is composed chiefly of white-collar workers and since its small business enterprises are insignificant in the American economy, the black bourgeoisie wields no political power as a class in American society. Nor does the black bourgeoisie exercise any significant power within the Negro community as an employer of labor. Its power within the Negro community stems from the fact that middle-class Negroes hold strategic positions in segregated institutions and create and propagate the ideologies current in the Negro community. (p. 86)

As will be shown, although desegregation has come quite a distance, the black bourgeoisie still has the same functional position.

8. In his book *Black Bourgeoisie*, E. F. Frazier highlights the Rosenwald Fund as a major example of northern industrial philanthropy.

9. For example, sociologist W. D. Rubinstein reports in *The Left, the Right, and the Jews*, published in 1982 by Universe Books, New York, that since 1945 almost the entire Jewish population in the United States and throughout the Western world has entered "the upper-middle class." The intraethnic class stratification among Jewish Americans thus stands in sharp contrast with that of black Americans (pp. 11–76).

10. See B. Woody and M. Malson, In Crisis: Low Income Black Employed Women in the U.S. Workplace, Working Paper No. 131, published by Wellesley College, Wellesley, MA, in 1984; and W. Darity, Jr., and S. L. Myers, Jr., Changes in Black Family Structure: Implications for Welfare Dependency, published in the *American Economic Review: AEA Papers and Proceedings*, May 1983.

11. See the substantial critical assessment of New Industrial Policy by R. McGahey and J. Jeffries in Employment, Training, and Industrial Policy: Implications for Minorities, a paper prepared for the Joint Center on Political

Studies Conference on Industrial Policy and Minority Economic Opportunity, October 13–14, 1983.

12. For a detailed analysis of the role of seniority arrangements and other union procedures as racially exclusionary tactics both in the public and private sector, see H. Hill, The Racial Practices of Organized Labor: The Contemporary Record, in J. Jacobson (Ed.), *The Negro and the American Labor Market*, published in 1968 by Anchor Books, Garden City, NY; H. Hill, The Equal Employment Opportunity Acts of 1964 and 1972: A Critical Analysis of the Legislative History and Administration of the Law, published in the *Industrial Relations Law Journal*, *2* (1) Spring 1977; and H. Hill, *Black Labor and the American Legal System*, published in 1986 by University of Wisconsin Press, Madison, WI.

13. In New York City six out of ten students do not complete high school in four years.

14. Data obtained from the University of Illinois at Chicago.

15. Data obtained from the University of North Carolina at Chapel Hill.

16. Of course, it is not clear when blacks as a group ever were "empowered" in the United States.

17. See D. K. Magner's article Decline in Doctorates Earned by Black and White Men Persists, Study Finds; Foreign Students and U.S. Women Fill Gaps, published March 1, 1989, in *The Chronicle of Higher Education.* In the same article, C. Smith, Dean of Graduate Studies at Florida A & M University, is quoted as observing that "the black male appears to be in a dangerous state of decline in both academics and society."

REFERENCES

Associated Press. (1987, December 29). Black enrollments in graduate schools drop, study says. *Durham Morning Herald*, p. 17A.

Bluestone, B., & Harrison, B. (1986, December). *The great American job machine: The proliferation of low wage employment in the U.S. economy*. Washington, DC: The Joint Economic Committee.

Bradbury, K. L., & Browne, L. E. (1986, March/April). Black men in the labor market. *New England Economic Review*, 32–42.

Brown, C. (1982). The federal attack on labor market discrimination: The mouse that roared. *Research in Labor Economics*, *5*, 60.

Brown, M. K., & Erie, S. P. (1981, Summer). Blacks and the legacy of the Great Society: The economic and political impact of federal social policy. *Public Policy*, 308–319.

Bunche, R. J. (1936, January). A critique of New Deal social planning as it affects Negroes. *Journal of Negro Education*, *62*, 65.

Clark, K.B., & Franklin, J. H. (1983). Foreword to *Policy framework for social justice*. Washington, DC: Joint Center for Political Studies.

Clark, L. H., Jr. (1986, December 4). Productivity's cost: Manufacturers grow much more efficient but employment lags. *The Wall Street Journal.*

Coe, R. D. (1974). A preliminary empirical examination of the dynamics of welfare use. *Analysis of the First Twelve Years of the Panel Study of Income Dynamics.* Ann Arbor: University of Michigan, Institute for Social Research.

Coe, R. D. (1982, September-October). Welfare dependence: Fact or myth? *Challenge, 25*(4), 43–49.

Coleman, M. (1983, December 4). More reliant on aid than whites, blacks hit hard by cuts. The *Washington Post,* p. A1, A18.

Darity, W., Jr. (1980, Winter). Illusions of black economic progress. *Review of Black Political Economy, 10,* 153–168.

Darity, W., Jr. (1983, November-December). The managerial class and surplus population. *Society, 21*(1), 54–62.

Darity, W., Jr. (1986, Spring). The managerial class and industrial policy. *Industrial Relations, 25*(2), 212–227.

Darity, W., Jr., & Myers, S. L., Jr. (1980, Summer). Changes in black-white income inequality, 1968–1978: A decade of progress? *Review of Black Political Economy, 10*(4), 355–374.

Darity, W., Jr., & Myers, S. L., Jr. (1984, Fall). Public policy and the condition of black family life. *Review of Black Political Economy, 13*(1–2), 165–187.

Duvall, J. (1987, October 31). New organization seeks to be voice of black professors. *The Carolina Times,* pp. 1, 4.

Frazier, E. F. (1957). *Black bourgeoisie: The rise of a new middle class in the United States.* Glencoe, IL: Free Press.

Freeman, R. B. (1973). Changes in the labor market for black Americans, 1948–72. *Brookings Papers on Economic Activity, 1.*

Freeman, R. B. (1986). Who escapes? The relation of church-going and other background factors to the socio-economic performance of black male youths from inner city poverty tracts. In R. B. Freeman (ed.), *The Black Youth Employment Crisis.* Chicago: University of Chicago Press.

Garg, D. (1986, December). *The impact of automation and computer-integrated manufacturing on industrial employment.* Paper presented at the annual meeting of the American Society of Mechanical Engineers.

Gomillion v. Lightfoot, 364 U.S. 399, 110 (1960).

Hogan, L. M. (1972, Fall). Review of Wilhelm's *Who Needs the Negro? Review of Black Political Economy, 3*(1).

Jacques-Garvey, A. (Ed.). (1969). *Philosophy and opinions of Marcus Garvey: Vols. I & II.* New York: Atheneum.

Leontief, W., & Duchin, F. (1986). *The future of automation on workers.* New York: Oxford University Press.

Mandel, E. (1980). *Long waves of capitalist development: The Marxist interpretation.* Cambridge: Cambridge University Press.

Marx, K. (1977). *Capital*, Vol. 1. New York: Vintage Books. (Originally published 1867.)

McGhee, J. D. (1982). *A dream denied: The black family in the eighties*. Washington, DC: National Urban League Research Department.

McLanahan, S. (1985). Family structure and reproduction of poverty. *American Journal of Sociology*, *90*, 873–901.

Michael, D. N. (1962). *Cybernation: The silent conquest*. Santa Barbara: Center for the Study of Democratic Institutions.

Nora, S., & Minc, A. (1978). *The computerization of society: A report to the president of France*. Cambridge, MA: MIT Press.

Rada, J. (1980). *The impact of micro-electronics: A tentative appraisal of information technology*. Geneva: International Labour Office.

Reis, D. (1987, May). Minorities on slow tenure track at Chicago area universities. *Chicago Reviewer*, 3–5.

Shaw, L. B. (1982). High school completions for young women: Impacts of low income and living with a single parent. *Journal of Family Issues*, *3*, 147–163.

Silberman, C. (1966). *The myths of automation*. New York: Harper Colophon Books.

Smith, J. P., & Welch, F. (1978, March). *Race differences in earnings: A survey and new evidence*. Santa Monica, CA: The Rand Corp.

Smith, J. P., & Welch, F. (1986, February). *Closing the gap: Forty years of economic progress for blacks*. Santa Monica: Rand Corporation.

Smith, J. P., & Welch, F. (1989, June). Black economic progress after Myrdal. *Journal of Economic Literature*, *27*(2), 519–564.

Taylor, P. A., Gwartney-Gibbs, P. A., & Farley, R. (1986). Changes in the structure of earnings inequality by race, sex, and industrial sector, 1960–80. *Research in Social Stratification and Mobility*, *5*, 105–138.

U.S. Bureau of the Census. (1983a). *Characterization of the population below the poverty level: 1981*. Current Population Reports Series P-60 No. 138. Washington, DC: U.S. Government Printing Office.

U.S. Bureau of the Census. (1983b). *Money income of households, families and persons in the United States: 1981*. Current Population Reports Series P-60 No. 137. Washington, DC: U.S. Government Printing Office.

Wilhelm, S. M. (1970). *Who needs the Negro?* Cambridge, MA: Schenkman Publishing.

Wilson, W. J. (1980). *The declining significance of race* (2nd ed.). Chicago: University of Chicago Press.

3

Black Political Participation: The Search for Power

E. Yvonne Moss, with Tobe Johnson, Dianne M. Pinderhughes, Michael B. Preston, Susan Welch, and John F. Zipp

Black political participation during the period 1940 to the present can be best understood as a search for power. Using both conventional and nonconventional politics, African-Americans sought inclusion, full participation, and effective representation in the nation's power centers and political arenas. Until the Voting Rights Act of 1965 secured the franchise for millions of African-Americans in the South and in some jurisdictions in the North and West, black political participation took unconventional forms including protests and political movements. Protests and demonstrations played a pivotal role in the political and social advancement of black Americans. African-Americans turned to these nonconventional political methods because the basic political relationship of black citizens to the polity was one of exclusion.

The politics of exclusion meant that African-Americans lacked access to political institutions and processes. Supreme Court interpretations of the Civil War Amendments to the Constitution and the civil rights laws and cases of the nineteenth century so emasculated these measures that black people were denied even the basic rights of citizenship that these amendments and laws were supposed to guarantee. Concomitantly, patterns of bias developed within the structures of politics that automatically disadvantaged black citizens (Harrigan, 1985; Fainstein & Fainstein, 1974; Katznelson, 1976, 1981). African-Americans were excluded from the power centers and bargaining arenas where public agendas were set and public policies determined. Disfranchisement in the South and dilution of power in both the North and West meant that the only avenues available for black political participation were accommodation, coalition, or confrontation (Carmichael & Hamilton, 1967; Greenberg, Milner, & Olson, 1971; Holden, 1973). The routine organization of race politics in the United States either excluded black participation or linked black citizens to the polity in a way that minimized their potential influence (Katznelson, 1976). Faced with a closed political system that was reinforced by de facto and de jure structures of segregation, African-Americans turned to agitation, litigation, and various nonviolent direct-action techniques to end segregation, second-class citizenship, and disfranchisement. The protests, demonstrations, and political violence of the sixties were the forms of political mobilizations that assumed importance after World War II (Greenberg, Milner, & Olson, 1971; Carson, 1981; Raines, 1983; Morris, 1984; Sears & McConahay, 1973; Miroff, 1979; Neiburg, 1969; Zinn, 1964).

Between 1940 and the late 1960s, the political aspirations of black Americans were expressed in mass popular movements for civil rights and for black power. The diverse group of leaders and organizations known collectively as the civil rights movement encompassed different political philosophies and orientations. Sometimes leaders and organizations initiated protest activity, but more often it was their role to give shape and direction to spontaneous popular sentiment and behavior (Morris, 1984; Raines, 1983; Carson, 1981). The civil rights movement was technically a sociopolitical movement in that it had both social and political objectives. As the emphasis shifted from the desegregation of public facilities to voter registration and political participation, there was an increasing awareness that finding solutions to social and economic ills required the gaining of political power (Carson, 1981; Carmichael & Hamilton, 1967; Meier, 1970; Breitman, 1967; King, 1968).

Prior to the emergence of the civil rights movement, terror and intimidation had long been used to reinforce economic, social, and political exclusion and domination.[1] Terror and intimidation were used to frighten African-Americans into acquiescence in and acceptance of the political order. Doctrines of white supremacy were a part of a political culture that justified exclusion on the basis of race. The brash militancy of some of the civil rights activists, the defiant and accusatory rhetoric of Malcolm X, the confrontational rhetoric of black power and the appeals to black nationalism, religious nationalism, and revolutionary nationalism, all functioned to counteract fear by generating a new group consciousness and identity. Issues of power and powerlessness were raised in both religious and secular terms. The political violence of the sixties, along with the black power movement, are direct reactions to the politics of exclusion (U.S.

Kerner Commission, 1968; Sears & McConahay, 1973; Neiburg, 1969; Button, 1978).

After 1965 black political mobilization was channeled more and more into electoral politics and conventional political behavior. Even so, nonconventional political activity—especially political movements—continued. Rent strikes and poor people's campaigns, the black power movement, urban political movements for community control, rural and urban movements for economic development and self-sufficiency, and political mobilization to elect black candidates are all examples of nonconventional political behavior on the part of black people in the late sixties and seventies (Altshuler, 1970; Lipsky, 1980; Fainstein & Fainstein, 1974; Piven & Cloward, 1977; James, 1973; Meier, 1970; Katznelson, 1981). Early campaigns to elect black mayors and other public officials relied to a considerable extent on nonconventional modes of political mobilization among black citizens.

Black political ascendancy and the transition to black rule in the cities has been the most visible result of black participation in conventional politics (Moss, 1977; Eisinger, 1980). However, progress in black empowerment is evident in other political arenas and levels of government as well. This chapter examines the gradual evolution of conventional black political participation, primarily through an evaluation of the developments in black registration and voting from the forties to the present. It also raises questions about the impact of increased black voting behavior and identifies the consequences of and the major issues associated with these developments. Additionally, the chapter discusses the political context of African-American politics, as well as pertinent theoretical issues regarding the structure of power.

The final section addresses the following questions: Why haven't increased black political participation, generally, and black political ascendancy in the cities, particularly, produced improvements in the economic and social lives of more African-Americans? What are the limits and what is the potential of political participation for the realization of black aspirations? What directions for political action are indicated by the study? And where do we go from here?

This chapter has a number of objectives: to review the trends in black registration and voting from 1940 to the present; to evaluate the impact and significance of black voting; to address the role and function of political movements; to examine the myths and realities of ideological differentiation in black populations; to describe the political context within which the search for power continues to take place; and to evaluate why this search continues. A discussion of context is critical because black

Table 3.1
Black Voter Registration in the South, 1940–1973

Year	Estimated Number of Registered Voters	Percentage of Black Voting Age Population
1940	250,000	5
1947	595,000	12
1952	1,008,614	20
1956	1,238,038	25
1960	1,414,052	28
1964	1,907,279	38
1968	3,312,000	62
1970	3,357,000	54
1971	3,488,565	59
1973	3,560,856	59

Source: Black Politics in the South, by D. Campbell and J. R. Feagin, 1975, *Journal of Politics, 37*, p. 133.

political activity takes place within the general structure and dynamics of American politics. Two key elements are the structure of race politics and the structure of power. Any comprehensive analysis of black politics and black political potential must take into consideration the relationship between black politics and the larger political context.

TRENDS IN BLACK REGISTRATION AND VOTING

In this section the trends in black registration and voting from 1940 to the present will be reviewed. One limitation of this project is that as we go back in time we have less information, so our trend data are incomplete and uneven. We do, however, have enough data to make some solid generalizations. The evidence on black registration, turnout, and vote preference will be discussed.

Table 3.1 presents data on black voter registration in the South from 1940 to 1973. One shortcoming of the registration data by race is that they are only available for the South. Several points are worth noting about this data. First, there was a 140% increase in black registration from 1940 to 1947, attributable largely to the ending of the white primary[2] (*Smith v. Allwright*) in 1944 (Walton, 1985). Second, black registration gains were steady, albeit slow, from 1947 until 1964, but there was a tremendous increase between 1964 and 1968, obviously a result of the passage of the Voting Rights Act of 1965.

A more detailed impact of this law can be seen in Table 3.2. This table contains voter registration figures for the South immediately prior to and after the Voting Rights Act. The table's only limitation for our purposes is that it lists these figures for whites and nonwhites, rather than whites and blacks. However, since blacks constituted the overwhelming number of nonwhites in these states, this is not a serious limitation. These results are quite clear: overall, nonwhite registration increased from 35.5% to 57.2% of the voting age population, an increase of over 60% in only a few years. Yet large gaps remain between nonwhite and white rates even after 1965. While the registration rate of whites in all southern states increased from 73.4% to only 76.5% prior to and after the Voting Rights Act of 1965, in 6 of the 11 southern states, whites registered at a rate approximately 30% higher than blacks. In one state, Tennessee, the percentage of increase in white voter registration was greater than that for blacks.

Since 1968 the U.S. Census Bureau has compiled registration and voting statistics broken down by various social groups for every national election. We have reproduced these for blacks and whites for the presidential elections from 1964 to 1984 (see Table 3.3). Black registration has remained remarkably stable through this period, starting out at 66.2% (1968), dropping in 1976 to 58.5%, but then rebounding to 66.3% in 1984. During the same time, white voter registration has decreased from 75.4% to 69.6%. Thus, the ratio of black registration to white registration increased from .88 to .95, an indication of the convergence of registration rates between blacks and whites.

Tables 3.3 and 3.4 contain figures on black voter turnout. In this presentation we are restricting our attention to voting in presidential elections because the greatest amount of information is available on these and they have been the most common focus of political analysts. For information on voting in other elections, see Hanes Walton's *Invisible Politics* (1985, chap. 5). The data in Table 3.3 come from the Census Bureau, while those in Table 3.4 are from the American National Election Studies Project (ANES) conducted by the University of Michigan. As has been discussed elsewhere (Wolfinger & Rosenstone, 1980), the estimates from these two sources disagree, with the ANES data tending to overreport voting. We ask the reader to bear this in mind when noting the differences between these two sets of results.

This having been said, the ANES data (Table 3.4) is the best for examining black turnout prior to 1968, even though it includes a relatively small number of blacks in each survey (Walton, 1985). From this data, we can see that black turnout in presidential elections hovered around 33% during the 1950s, increased dramatically to 52.9% in 1960 and then to

Table 3.2

Voter Registration in the South, Prior to and After the Voting Rights Act of 1965

State	Pre-Act Registration Percentage		% Point	Post-Act Registration Percentage		% Point
	White	Nonwhite	Difference[a]	White	Nonwhite	Difference[a]
Alabama	69.2	19.3	49.9	89.6	51.6	38.0
Arkansas	65.5	40.4	25.1	72.4	62.8	9.6
Florida	74.8	51.2	23.6	81.4	63.6	17.6
Georgia	62.6	27.4	35.2	80.3	52.6	27.7
Louisiana	80.5	31.6	48.9	93.1	58.9	34.2
Mississippi	69.9	6.7	63.2	91.5	59.8	31.7
North Carolina	96.8	46.8	50.0	83.0	51.3	31.7
South Carolina	75.7	37.3	38.4	81.7	51.2	30.5
Tennessee	72.9	69.5	3.4	80.6	71.7	8.9
Texas	....	....	....	53.3	61.6	-8.3
Virginia	61.1	38.3	22.8	63.4	55.6	7.8
Total	73.4	35.5	37.9	76.5	57.2	19.3

[a]Prepared by author.

Source: *Political Participation* (pp. 222-23), by U.S. Commission on Civil Rights, 1968, Washington, DC: Government Printing Office.

Table 3.3
National Registration and Voting by Race, 1964–1984

	1964	1968	1972	1976	1980	1984
Blacks						
Percentage of voting-age population reported registered	NA	66.2%	65.5%	58.5%	60.0%	66.3%
Percentage of voting-age population reported voting	58.5%	57.6%	52.1%	48.7%	50.5%	55.8%
Whites						
Percentage of voting-age population reported registered	NA	75.4%	73.4%	68.3%	68.6%	69.6%
Percentage of voting-age population reported voting	70.7%	69.1%	64.5%	60.9%	61.1%	61.4%

Source: *Current Population Reports, Special Studies*, U.S. Bureau of the Census, Series P-23, No. 131.

Table 3.4
Reported Voter Turnout by Race for Presidential Elections, 1952–1984

	1952	1956	1960	1964	1968	1972	1976	1980	1984
White	78.5	76.5	81.9	79.6	77.1	73.8	72.5	72.3	75.2
Black	33.1	34.9	52.9	64.9	67.7	64.7	65.0	66.7	65.6

Source: Data for 1952 to 1978 from *American National Election Studies Data Sourcebook, 1952-1978* (p. 317), by W.E. Miller, A.H. Miller, and E.J. Schneider; 1980, Cambridge: Harvard University Press. Data for 1980, 1982, and 1984 from American National Election Studies, Center for Political Studies, University of Michigan.

Table 3.5
Percent Democratic Vote in Presidential Elections, 1952–1984

	1952	1956	1960	1964	1968	1972	1976	1980	1984
Blacks	80	64	71	100	97	87	95	86	91
Whites	40	39	48	65	41	30	47	36	33

Source: Data for 1952 to 1976 from *American National Election Studies Data Sourcebook, 1952-1978*, by W.E. Miller, A.H. Miller, and E.J. Schneider; 1980, Cambridge: Harvard University Press. Data for 1980 to 1984 cited in *The Social Basis of Politics* by A.K. Sherman and A. Kolker, 1987, Belmont, CA: Wadsworth.

64.9% in 1964, and has remained relatively stable since then. This masks the change in the South, however, where turnout among blacks increased from 4% in 1952 to 31% in 1960 and 63% in 1968 (Cassel, 1979). Similar trends, although at lower levels of reported voting, are found in the census data (Table 3.3).

In addition to the data on turnout, we have figures on the presidential preferences of blacks. Most of this data is based on the ANES surveys, and therefore covers only the period from 1952 to 1984 (see Table 3.5). What we know about black voting from 1940 until 1948 indicates that blacks voted overwhelmingly Democratic during these three elections (Glantz, 1960). And, as is well-known and is documented in Table 3.5, this trend has continued to the present. Essentially, the conclusion that can be drawn from the turnout and preference data is that in presidential elections blacks either vote Democrat or do not vote at all.

The increases in black participation in electoral politics should be viewed within a political context in which there have been major barriers to registration and voting. Any impediment to registration, obviously enough, is also an impediment to voting. The reverse is not true, however. Even when black citizens are registered, obstacles to effective and meaningful voting can be devised (e.g., racial gerrymandering; see Parker, 1984). During these years between 1940 and 1987 there were five general types of barriers used to inhibit full participation of black voters in electoral contests. These included legal or procedural barriers, illegal barriers, the effects of socioeconomic status, psychological factors and organizational factors, and the residual consequences of the political culture. Legal or procedural barriers include pre-1965 mechanisms that resulted in disfranchisement, such as the white primary, poll taxes, and literacy tests. Since 1965 other methods have been used to discourage registration and voting among African-Americans, including difficult registration requirements; frequent purges of registration rolls; moving polling places with little or no notice; and reducing the number of polling places within black residential areas (Davidson, 1984, p. 3).

One illustration of the impact of registration rules is evident from Wolfinger and Rosenstone's study *Who Votes?* (1980). Based on 1972 data they estimated that if all states had registration procedures as simple and accessible as the most liberal state, turnout for whites would have increased by 8.9% and for blacks by 11.3%. It is apparent that the nature and type of registration requirements employed in the United States depresses the turnout of blacks more than that of whites.

After the passage of the Voting Rights Act in 1965 the key question was no longer whether African-Americans could participate in conventional politics, but rather what the terms of that participation would be. Since 1965 the kinds of limitations on black political participation used during the machine era in northern and midwestern cities (Katznelson, 1976) have been increasingly used in other jurisdictions to constrain black political potential. Just as the structure of race politics during the machine era (in places like New York and Chicago) and during the progressive era (Fainstein & Fainstein, 1974; Harrigan, 1985) limited the effectiveness of black political participation, so after 1965 in the South, new mechanisms were tried to limit the political potential of black voters who registered and began voting in record numbers.

Other mechanisms do not actually prevent blacks from voting, but rather dilute the political impact of the black vote (Bell, 1980). Since the importance of one's vote increases turnout (Zipp, 1985), these mechanisms have the effect of being an obstacle to effective black voting. These obstacles have become more important since the Voting Rights Act of 1965 eliminated many of the outright barriers to actual participation by blacks. These methods include at-large elections, gerrymandering, anti-single shot devices, annexation of predominantly white areas, and runoff requirements that stipulate that no candidate can be elected without 50% of the vote (Davidson, 1984; Davidson & Korbel, 1981; Parker, 1984; Walton, 1985). From 1964 to 1975, 20 county governments and boards of education changed from district-based to at-large elections (Voter Education Project, 1976). Many of these changes occurred in southern states (Davidson, 1984, pp. 11–12).

The effects of these changes on minority vote dilution can be assessed by drawing on Davidson and Korbel's (1981) study of political units in Texas that changed from at-large to ward-based systems during the 1970s. They found that the number of elected officials who were African-American or Mexican-American was three times greater under ward-based systems. Furthermore, there is evidence that southern states covered by the Voting Rights Act have increasingly requested the sorts of changes in electoral procedures (at-large elections, annexations, changes in polling places) that dilute black voting strength, and that there is a positive relationship between the number of black elected officials and the number of such requests (D. H. Hunter, 1974; U.S. Commission on Civil Rights, 1982). Similarly, southern states have often failed to submit these changes for preclearance, as is required by law. The U.S. Commission on Civil Rights concluded that there were over 500 election law changes that were not submitted for preclearance in Alabama, Georgia, and Mississippi alone (Simpson & Yinger, 1985, p. 231). In some states (Georgia, Mississippi, and South Carolina), when requests for such changes were denied, state officials managed to implement them through other means (Davidson, 1984, p. 12).

Illegal barriers to both registration and voting have also been used to restrict the use of the franchise by black citizens. The history of these barriers prior to 1965 is well-known and includes such things as the threat and/or use of violence, economic harm, verbal abuse, and, most prevalently, arbitrary registration procedures (e.g., the closing of doors as soon as blacks attempted to register). Investigations by the U.S. Commission on Civil Rights concluded that such discriminatory practices were concentrated in 129 counties in 10 southern states (U.S. Commission on Civil Rights, 1959, 1961).

After 1965, local southern officials continued to erect roadblocks to black registration and voting. Frequently the same white registrars who were hostile to blacks prior to the Voting Rights Act remained in office after its passage. Again, arbitrary procedures were used to hinder blacks. Registration places were changed, and blacks were purged from registration rolls without notice. Posted office hours were not kept. If blacks did register, they faced problems in actually voting. Common practices included failing to list the black voter on the precinct list or, if listed, failing to locate his or her name on election day; harassing black voters when they tried to cast their ballots; and refusing to allow blacks to vote without verification of their eligibility from city hall (U.S. Commission on Civil Rights, 1975).

Conventional wisdom dictates that higher socioeconomic status (SES) is positively related to voting (Milbrath & Goel, 1977). The argument is that a person with a higher SES is better integrated into society, has a better education which allows for more effective processing of political information, and is more aware of the need for and the benefits of political participation (Lipset, 1963; Verba & Nie, 1972). Contrary to these conventional concepts, black citizens with low SES are more likely to vote than whites with low SES (Olsen, 1970; Verba & Nie, 1972, pp. 170–171). Two different explanations have been offered for this. One is that blacks are more "group conscious" than whites and that this consciousness moves blacks to participate in politics (Verba & Nie, 1972, pp. 158–159). A second explanation holds that blacks are more tied to the community and that this tie prompts political participation (Olsen, 1970). The work of Danigelis (1978), who tested these assumptions, and Walton (1985) indicates that it is primarily structural factors that influence black voter turnout. The most important of these is the "political climate"—whether the electoral structure is supportive, intolerant, or indifferent in respect to black political participation. Black voters turn out in higher numbers regardless of SES when they have something or someone to vote for and when structural factors are not a barrier to voting.

It is not clear what role psychological factors such as fear, apathy, and deference to whites—which historically have had an impact on black voting patterns—have today (Salaman & Van Evera, 1973; Kernell, 1973). Organizational factors, however, are clearly related to black registration and voting. The reluctance of political parties to nominate and support black candidates for office has a chilling effect on black participation. On the other hand, the presence of black candidates and federal registrars is significantly related to black political mobilization (Walton, 1985, p. 76). Voters' perceptions that a particular candidate represents their interests increases turnout (Zipp, 1985). And in city races the presence of black mayoral candidates increases black voter turnouts (Morris, 1984). In presidential politics, Jesse Jackson's bid for the Democratic nomination generally increased black registration and voting (Reed, 1986). For example, in Alabama, there was an 87% increase; in New York, the increase was a dramatic 127%.

Historically, the evolution of a political culture that legitimized the exclusion of African-Americans from the political life of the country politically neutralized black citizens (Walton, 1985). With disfranchisement black people lost more than the right to vote. What was also lost were the political benefits that accrue from suffrage rights, such as employment opportunities and the improvement of schools and services. In 1880 African-Americans were a majority in 300 counties in the United States. By 1970 that number was down to 100. It is interesting to surmise what the impact on black life might have been if political inclusion rather than political exclusion had been the norm in American politics from the 1880s onward.

IMPACT ON BLACK VOTING

While the impact of black registration and voting during the years 1940 to 1987 has been considerable, controversy remains over whether greater participation in politics can change the material conditions of most African-Americans. The Voting Rights Act of 1965 created the opportunity for millions of black people to register and vote without harassment, threats, or fears of reprisals. This accomplishment is of historical importance because for the first time in the nation's history black Americans began to enjoy some of the benefits of citizenship. Black voters have helped to elect blacks to public office, as well as whites who are sympathetic to black interests. Even though black elected officials (BEOs) represented only 1.2% of the total number of elected officials in the United States (490,770) in 1984, there was a 300% increase in the number of BEOs between 1970 and 1985, from 1,469 to 6,065 (Williams, 1987). While there were fewer than 300 BEOs in the country in 1965, by 1987 there were 6,681 (Boamah-Wiafe, 1990).

These gains, however, are not reflected at all levels of government. The greatest inroads have been at the county level, while the election of black candidates to state offices has been the least successful. Virginia's recent election of the nation's first black elected governor was, therefore, especially historic. At this writing there are no black representatives in the U.S. Senate and only a few in Congress. In addition to the nation's one black governor, there are a few state officials who are black. Some of the nation's black members of Congress, as well as black lobbying organizations and black party officials, have gained positions of influence in American political institutions. Even so, some scholars conclude that electoral success has not located black Americans in real positions of power.

In recent years the number of BEOs has declined. Since traditionally the most critical determinant of electoral success is the percentage of blacks voting in a district—the election of BEOs in districts with black people representing less than 40% of the population is not common—the number of blacks elected to office would seem to be limited by the number of majority or near-majority black districts in the United States. There is, however, evidence to support the conclusion that the presence of black voters makes an impact even when black officeholders are not elected. A sizable block of black voters influences the political agendas of candidates and elected officials. For example, there was a decline in the segregationist rhetoric in southern gubernatorial races after the increase in black voter participation (Black, 1976). Concomitantly, white members of Congress who have a sizable black population in their districts have been supporters of civil rights legislation (Bass & DeVries, 1976; Feagin, 1972).

While the election of black officials, especially big-city mayors, is a limited political resource for addressing certain kinds of political issues—like the economic inequality between blacks and whites—BEOs have had some positive impact on the distribution of services to black members of the polity. One of these areas is the increase in the proportion of black municipal employment. In a study of 40 cities, Eisinger (1983) concluded that the presence of a black mayor was one of the most important reasons for the growth of black municipal employment in the 1970s. In his study of Durham, North Carolina, and Tuskegee, Alabama, Keech (1968) found that black voting resulted in greater black public employment and a fairer distribution of public services. Similar conclusions concerning the positive impact of black elected officials have been reported by Campbell and Feagin (1975), Coombs, Alsikafi, Bryan, and Webber (1977), Greer (1979), Karnig and Welch (1980), and Marshall and Tabb (1985).

Some argue that increases in black municipal employment have primarily benefitted members of the black middle class. Additionally, the increase in black political power in major cities in the United States has taken place at a time when the power of cities to affect significant changes in the social structure has decreased (Williams, 1987). Changes in urban political structures have limited the power of city government officials to effect social change. Black mayors are not able to provide the benefits to their constituents that ethnic mayors in political machines traditionally were able to provide. Thus, participation does not bring the power it once did to affect issues of social mobility. Despite the limitations inherent in the contemporary organization of politics in the United States, both the dramatic increase in the number of BEOs since 1965 and the transition to black rule in the nation's largest cities denote critical rather than routine changes in the structure of racial politics in America.[3]

Voting by itself is a limited political resource. The fact that over 6,209,000 black Americans remained unregistered in 1987 further limits voting potential. Nevertheless, black voters are becoming more sophisticated in utilizing the power of the vote to reward friends and to punish enemies whether they are black or white. Although the actual black registration and voter turnout lags behind the potential, scholars still find reason for optimism. The gap between voter registration rates for black and white citizens narrowed to 3.3% points in 1984 from 9.2% points in 1968 (see Table 3.3). The gap in voter turnout narrowed from 10.4% points in 1980 to 5.6% points in 1984 (see Table 3.3). The steady increase in the numbers of BEOs since 1965 is likely to increase even with a limited number of majority black districts. Such an increase is possible if black candidates capture larger shares of the votes of other racial groups (including whites), if black voter registration and turnout is increased, and if the structural barriers to effective political participation among African-Americans are reduced or eliminated.

There has been a long-standing debate concerning voting as a source of social change. Is social change best accomplished by devoting one's energies to electing candidates who represent one's interests, or is it best to remain outside the electoral arena and use one's resources to build social movements or to engage in related activities (Piven & Cloward, 1977)? This debate has had a long history within the black movement. Some analysts have questioned whether social problems could ever be solved through the vote (e.g., Brown, 1969; Jones, 1972; Greenberg, Milner, & Olson, 1971). On the other hand, Dr. Martin Luther King, Jr., said in 1965 that if blacks could vote "there would be no oppressive poverty directed against Negroes, our children would not be crippled by segregated schools, and the whole community might live together in harmony" (Herbers, 1965). Other writers (Greeley, 1971; Levy & Kramer, 1972) have voiced similar positions. Perhaps the safest conclusion is to point out the debate and to note that voting, by itself, has limited political power.

Focusing only on conventional political participation may also be misleading because central to any analysis of black politics is the general question of politics and power.[4] Many political and social scientists have studied political participation from the pluralist viewpoint. The assumption is that voting has a substantial impact not only on who holds office but also on public policy. It is further assumed that the range of issues subject to debate by elected officials is not significantly narrower than all the concerns that confront a given polity. This view ignores the fact that some issues never come up for debate (Bachrach & Baratz, 1970). Those who hold the power of nondecisions in public agenda-setting often do not hold public office, are little known to the public, and are seldom accountable to public interests (Bachrach & Baratz, 1962). As Alford and Friedland (1975) noted, some groups (e.g., the upper classes) have power without participating in politics, while others (e.g., the lower classes) can actively participate yet not have power.

Schattschneider (1960), Dolbeare and Edelman (1981), Katznelson and Kesselman (1987), Greenberg (1986), Parenti (1970b, 1983), F. Hunter (1953), Mills (1956), and Dye (1979) all contradict and call into question the pluralist model of politics and power in America. And, even if one accepts the pluralist model, there are built-in limits and impediments to full participation by black citizens in conventional pluralist politics (Greenberg, Milner, & Olson, 1971). Greenberg's comments made almost 20 years ago have contemporary applicability:

> Recall that under the pluralist model some questions remain outside the boundaries of legitimate political discourse and decision making. Communities seem to reach a decision, whether explicitly or implicitly, that some concerns and related solutions are not proper subject matter for the political arena. Unfortunately, many questions considered closed by the majority of the community are often of vital importance to Black citizens. William Keech, for example, in his excellent study of the impact of Negro voting [1968], . . . has suggested that problems for Black people that are based in the private sector or the economy or are derivative from past discriminatory practices are not only difficult to rectify, but are difficult to raise for public discussion in the first place. Thus, proposals to radically alter the social and economic situation of the Black population are not raised, nor are serious efforts made to alter discrimination in housing or in jobs. In short, many issues that are vitally necessary to the health and well being of Black citizens are often not considered sufficiently compelling or legitimate to reach the public agenda. (pp. 11–12)

This exclusion of issues vital to black interests forced African-Americans to use alternative political forms in the post–World War II era, "including confrontation, disruption, and violence" (Greenberg, Milner, & Olson, 1971, p. iii). After the passage of the Voting Rights Act in 1965, black people began participating in large numbers in conventional political activities. Conventional politics alone, however, has not allowed African-Americans to overcome the politics of exclusion. Consequently, nonconventional political activity, including popular political movements, became an important vehicle for the expression of black political aspirations.

POLITICAL MOVEMENTS

Black churches and community organizations, which provide the permanent infrastructure of black political movements, have figured prominently in the successful candidacies of African-Americans. Astute black politicians have long used community, social, and fraternal organizations as reliable means to mobilize black citizens. The mayoral campaigns of Harold Washington (Chicago) and Mel King (Boston) illustrate the importance of community organizations and mass mobilization in conventional political contests (Holli & Green, 1984; Jennings & King, 1986; Bush, 1984). Additionally, Jennings suggests that activists who were associated primarily with nonconventional political activity in the past have begun to participate in conventional electoral contests, bringing with them a third ideological orientation (Jennings, 1990). These "black empowerment activists" challenge the traditional orientations of black politicians in conventional politics. The development of black political leadership through union organizing and labor politics (Widick, 1972) and the successful election campaigns of black candidates considered to be on the political left, like Kenneth Cockrel (Georgakas & Surkin, 1975; Bush, 1984), illustrate this phenomenon. Nonconventional politics and popular political movements have been significant in the recruitment and training of black leadership as well as the articulation and dissemination of new political ideas. Political movements further provide important linkages between citizens' interests and organizations.

The theory of comparative advantage is used to explain the different roles and activities that various community groups carry out in political movements and electoral campaigns. Groups like the National Urban League and the NAACP reach their particular clienteles. Political activists target new clientele groups. Black newspapers and radio stations keep the political message alive. Social and fraternal organizations and black churches spread the message, solicit volunteers, and raise funds. Churches in particular have carried out important political functions. They provide arenas wherein groups with different orientations come together to create common goals. Churches act as intermediaries for political parties. Black churches also function as centers for political mobilization, either for specific campaigns or on a continuous basis. Political leaders have historically been recruited and developed from among black clergy. Indeed, black ministers have played varied and significant roles in electoral politics and in programs for economic development.

The direct and indirect political roles that black ministers have carried out include providing access for politicians to their congregations, mobilizing church members for mass protests or elections, and running for political office themselves or acting as power brokers for those who do. The Reverend Jesse Jackson's candidacy for the Democratic party nomination for president in 1984 and 1988 was one of the most striking new political developments in American politics in recent years (Barker & Walters, 1989). Jackson's bid represented the first time the possibility of an African-American president began to be taken seriously.

Black participation in presidential and local political campaigns has provided interesting information about how to activate the "unmotivated" voter. "Unmotivated" voters are mobilized to participate in politics because of the potential for success of a candidate or cause, and because the process itself encourages the development of a sense of personal empowerment. Group motivation influences black voters as well as individual motivation. Political movements are products of incremental political experiences. Earlier protests have helped people to move from passive to active participation. Scholars note that the policy choices and attitudes of black citizens who do not vote are quite different from those who do, although what these differences are is not clear. An examination of black public opinion provides some clarity on ideological issues.

IDEOLOGICAL DIFFERENCES IN BLACK PUBLIC OPINION

There has been widespread publicity given to speculation that conservatism has been growing among African-Americans, and especially among those in the middle class, which has grown from approximately 5% in 1955 to 33% in 1985 (Thompson, 1974; Parent & Stekler, 1985; Farley, 1984). Evidence does not support this speculation, although the presumption that the black middle class is more conservative than the black lower class is understandable. Even though black people share a common experience of oppression, subordination, and discrimination based on race, scholars have noted distinct class differences (McClean, 1984; Johnson & Roark, 1984; Baker, 1964; Frazier, 1939, 1957; Myrdal, 1944; Drake & Cayton, 1962; Pettigrew, 1964; Moynihan, 1972). While the focus of the distinction was often on sociological traits—such as patterns of consumption, religious values, and voluntary association membership—or on physical traits—such as skin color, researchers noted important political differences as well. For example, an examination of the black elite in 1940 found that 50% of those from the North and almost 80% of those from other regions were still Republican when the party allegiance of the majority of the black masses had shifted to Roosevelt and the Democrats (McBride & Little, 1981; Sites & Mullins, 1985). Class differences were also significant in black support for Marcus Garvey's United Negro Improvement Association in the post–World War I years (Franklin, 1967) and for the Nation of Islam in the 1960s. In our society social class is a key predictor of all sorts of behavior, including political beliefs and actions (Milbrath & Goel, 1977; Thompson, 1974; Parent & Stekler, 1985; see also occupational distributions of blacks reported in Farley, 1984). What is surprising is that given all the speculation about an increase in black conservatism there is little empirical evidence to document it, though to be sure a few black conservatives have achieved considerable notoriety.

Evidence regarding intrablack attitudinal differences is fragmentary. In national surveys sample populations contain very small numbers of African-Americans. For example, a random sample of 1,500 Americans, the standard number surveyed in major opinion polls, contains only 180 African-Americans. While such a number is sufficient to say something about black attitudes in general, it is hardly enough to make detailed analysis of differences based on income, eduction, or other indices of class.

During the past two decades national surveys focused specifically on blacks have occasionally been conducted, such as those done by the Survey Research Center at the University of Michigan in 1984 and the Gallup and Joint Center for Political Studies in 1984. Even so, few reliable studies of black opinion have been published. An examination of published studies yields the following insights. Using the two traditional ways of measuring ideological preference—self-identification and reaction to specific issues—researchers found that few black persons consider themselves to be ideologically conservative (Welch & Foster, 1987). Only 15% of those interviewed in the 1984 Gallup/Joint Center survey placed themselves in the three most conservative positions on a 10-point scale; while 34% placed themselves on the three most liberal positions. On average blacks were 1.2 points more liberal than whites.

Additionally, in reaction to social welfare issues (government spending more money on health, education, welfare, and social issues) black respondents were more liberal than white respondents overall, at all income levels. The liberal gap was greatest among respondents with higher incomes (Gilliam & Whitby, 1987; Parent & Stekler, 1985; Welch & Foster, 1987). On race issues, black citizens were more favorable than white citizens were to busing, affirmative action, and government spending to help African-Americans. There are few studies of black opinion on abortion and school prayer issues. From what is available on black attitudes on these "morality issues," African-Americans are more conservative than white Americans on mandatory school prayer, abortion, and women's rights—except ERA (Secret, Johnson, & Welch, 1986; Seltzer & Smith, 1985; Ransford & Miller, 1983; Granberg & Granberg, 1980; Welch & Combs, 1983, 1985; Hall & Ferree, 1986). However, blacks are more opposed to the death penalty and more likely to favor gun control than whites (Combs & Comer, 1982; Seltzer & Smith, 1985).

One would expect that a conservative self-identification would be accompanied by advocacy of conservative positions on issues. This is true among whites, although the relationship between identification and activism is not strong. However, a recent study among blacks found that conservative self-identification is almost totally unrelated to conservatism on social welfare spending (Welch & Foster, 1987). Self-declared black conservatives were as likely to take the same liberal positions as black liberals, except on moral issues. Even among highly educated blacks, self-identification and issue-position are not related.

Like other Americans, it appears that blacks became slightly more conservative during the 1970s and early 1980s (Welch & Combs, 1983, 1985; Gilliam & Whitby, 1987). However, blacks moved less far to the right than did whites, especially the white upper classes. There is little solid data on the extent of the black shift to the right during this period for two reasons: a lack of comparability of samples over time; and, where such samples are available, a lack of sufficient numbers of black respondents to make reliable estimates.

On social welfare issues, Welch and Combs (1983, 1985) found few differences among African-Americans of different social classes among the small numbers of black people sampled in several National Opinion Research Center (NORC) General Social Surveys. Middle-class blacks were less likely than lower-class blacks to support federal welfare programs, but they were more liberal in supporting federal programs for health and education. Seltzer and Smith (1985) present similar findings from the 1982 NORC data, using education as an indication of social status (cf. Caldwell, 1978). Parent and Stekler (1985), who used small samples of blacks from the Survey Research Center's National Election Studies, also found middle-class blacks less likely than other blacks to support federal guarantees for jobs and standards of living. Additionally, Gilliam and Whitby (1987) also found the black middle class slightly more conservative than the lower class on the use of public spending to solve a variety of social and economic problems. Using a much larger sample (over 1,000 blacks and 1,400 whites) from the Joint Center/Gallup 1984 election polls, Welch and Foster (1987) found that blacks of higher income are less enthusiastic about social welfare spending than lower-income blacks. The class differences, however, were less than those among whites. Gilliam and Whitby (1987) also found class differences considerably less pronounced among blacks than among whites.

What is clear from available though fragmentary data is that patterns of public opinion among African-Americans do not fit easily into the traditional typologies used to explain patterns of white American public opinion. Although the black middle class is somewhat more conservative than the black lower classes, when considered in terms of income group overall, blacks are substantially more liberal than whites. The black middle class is more liberal relative to the white middle class than is the black lower class to the white lower class. The class differences among African-Americans are much smaller than in the white community. When comparing intraracial ideological patterns, it appears that members of the black middle class are somewhat more conservative on social welfare issues than black citizens with lower SES, but less conservative on race and morality issues.

Parent and Stekler (1985) show that middle-class blacks are more likely than lower-class blacks to assert that civil rights progress is too slow and less likely to agree that there has been a lot of change in civil rights. They are also more likely than lower-class blacks to say they identify closely with other blacks. On the other hand, Bolce and Gray (1979), in interviews with 600 New York City residents, discovered that lower-class blacks were more supportive of affirmative action than were higher status blacks.

Others have found few consistent class differences in support of race issues (Welch & Foster, 1987). The safest generalization to make concerning class differences in the black community regarding civil rights and race issues is that there is no clearcut difference in attitudes. Such a conclusion is not surprising given that on issues of racial and legal subordination blacks have historically been treated as if class did not matter.

On moral issues intraracial differences have been examined less frequently but, as in attitudes toward racial issues, there is certainly no evidence that the black middle class is more conservative than the lower class (Welch & Foster, 1987; Seltzer & Smith, 1985). On certain issues, such as abortion, sex education, drug education, homosexuality, and birth control, the black middle class is probably more liberal than their lower-income and less-educated peer group (Seltzer & Smith, 1985; Hall & Feree, 1986). On the other hand, middle-class blacks, especially men, are more conservative in their attitudes toward the roles of women than are other blacks (Ransford & Miller, 1983).

In terms of gender, black women are more likely to vote Democratic than black men (Bolce, 1985). One study examining four general issues (social welfare, military spending, traditional moral values, and affirmative action) found that while women were more opposed to military spending, there were no significant sex differences on the other issues (Welch & Foster, 1987). One study of attitudes toward support for a woman for president found black women more supportive than black men (Sigelman & Welch, 1984).

In conclusion, there is not much evidence of a new black conservatism. Furthermore, on issues other than social welfare, there is no evidence whatsoever that the black middle class is more conservative than the black lower class. Indeed, on many race and morality issues, the middle class is more liberal. In the overall spectrum of American politics, middle-class blacks are quite liberal.

POLITICAL EXCLUSION, POLITICAL POWER, AND BLACK POLITICS

The political relationship of African-Americans to the polity from 1619 through the colonial period and since 1776 has been one of powerlessness. This fundamental political relationship took variant forms in 1865 and in 1877 and during the Great Migration to the urban North and West from 1894 to 1914, but did not change. Social and economic issues important to black citizens could not be placed on the public policy agenda because of the structure of racial politics, specifically disfranchisement and dilution.

Politically almost completely subordinated in the South, African-Americans at the turn of the century turned to the accommodationist politics of Booker T. Washington (Katznelson, 1976; Holden, 1973). By 1915, however, even Washington supporters were disillusioned by the response of the Republican party to black aspirations. New organizations, including the NAACP, pioneered different strategies to advance black interests. The ways in which black citizens were linked to the polity in northern cities during the machine era provided participation without representation and power. Black political activities were controlled and directed by the bosses of urban political machines (Katznelson, 1976, 1981). Progressive politics and the New Deal brought reform to local and national governmental structures. With regard to African-American citizens, however, the changes were largely symbolic; there was no substantial inclusion in the political process (Fainstein & Fainstein, 1974; Harrigan, 1985). Improvements that did occur in black life during the New Deal were largely linked to the general improvements experienced by all Americans because of the policies of FDR's administration. And in many locales, relief was still distributed in a segregated and discriminatory manner (Mayor LaGuardia's Commission, 1969).

A. Philip Randolph's "March on Washington" movements in 1941 and 1942 began the active phase of the modern civil rights movement. The creation of the Federal Employment Practices Commission, the desegregation of war industries, and in 1949 the desegregation of the armed forces were all consequences of an emerging mass movement. The Supreme Court decision in *Brown* (1954) and the victories in the Montgomery bus boycott (1955–56) were historical catalysts for the explosive direct-action campaigns that accelerated in the late 1950s, and for the student movement in the early 1960s. These sociopolitical movements confronted and challenged the nation's century-old practices and laws promoting racial and political subordination of African-Americans.

The modern civil rights movement (since 1940) began as an attempt to improve black life by seeking a more just society (the "beloved community," see Carson, 1981; McAdam, 1988). The objectives of the movement were as much philosophical, religious, moral, and social as they were political. Moral appeals often elicited moral responses from Americans as individuals and from private groups. But the pragmatic realities of the American political and decision-making structure resulted in a very slow change in government policy (Miroff, 1979). The apparent reluctance of the federal government to protect the constitutional rights of black citizens led to disillusionment among many activists.

Some sectors of the civil rights movement became politicized and radicalized. Politics was viewed as the best hope for getting black concerns onto public policy agendas. Countervailing power was viewed as the best means to protect black life and interests. Those who took the political promises of the American creed to heart—like the members of the Mississippi Freedom Democratic party in 1964—did not realize the constraints inherent in the American political system. Others—equating the status of black Americans with that of colonized peoples around the globe—advocated far-reaching changes in the American political system. For those who pursued power within conventional politics, the built-in limits to what could be accomplished in the public arena meant that even after the transition to black rule in many jurisdictions, black empowerment remained illusive.

Until 1965 the basic thrust of black political efforts was a search for power, that is, a struggle to influence the authoritative decisions that affected black lives. In legislation, litigation, coalitions, accommodation, and confrontation, in demonstrations and mobilizations of public opinion, the goal was always power and influence. Disfranchisement, dilution, and the structure of racial politics were the major barriers to the acquisition of power. Politics, conventional and nonconventional, were viewed as a means to overcome this politics of exclusion. Structural barriers to black political participation were lowered though not eliminated by the Voting

Rights Act (1965) and decisions in *Gomillion* (1960) and other dilution cases (Bell, 1980). However, even after dramatic increases in black participation, along with success in electoral and conventional politics, the search for power continues. The most salient question is why.

There are three major reasons why the search for power is far from over: the limits and constraints of our constitutional government (e.g., federalism and the Dillon rule); political change in the structures of urban and national government; and the overall structure of power in America. Public power in the United States is fragmented and dispersed at the national level into separate institutions—none of which can make and implement policy without the positive action of others. This fragmentation and dispersal of public policy-making authority necessitates deal making, compromise, and incrementalism. The function of these devices has been to make it difficult for any elected faction to gain a majority and directly exercise popular will. The fear was not the tyranny of the despot but the tyranny of the crowd (Parenti, 1983; Greenberg, 1986).

Additionally, federalism grants power to both the national and the state governments. One example of the consequences of this system was the decision of the state of Mississippi in the Neshoba County murders (Bell, 1980, pp. 216–218) not to prosecute the defendants for the murders of three civil rights workers, James E. Chaney, Andrew Goodwin, and Michael H. Schwerner. The only legal recourse available when the state declined to bring criminal charges against local sheriffs and 15 other assailants was for the federal government to charge the assailants with the violation of the victims' civil rights. In this case, the federal structure did not give jurisdiction to the national government to indict those convicted under the civil rights statutes for murder.

The Dillon rule made the autonomy and existence of cities and towns dependent on state legislatures (Goodall & Sprengel, 1975).[5] While states do grant home-rule charters that increase the autonomy of large cities and municipalities, these charters can be changed or revoked at any time. Thus in Detroit and Atlanta when African-American mayors were first elected the city charters were changed to limit each mayor's tenure to two terms.[6]

Changes in urban and national political structures also contributed to the politics of exclusion. From about 1900 to the early 1930s (later in some jurisdictions, like Chicago), urban political machines, geographically based in white ethnic communities, dominated urban political life in northern cities. These machines were able to provide their ethnic constituencies with material rewards in exchange for solid political support at the polls. There is considerable debate over whether ethnic political machines provided anything more than symbolic political rewards or whether the ability of ethnic political bosses to broker for the substantive interest of their constituencies was co-opted by more powerful political and economic elites (Katznelson, 1981). Also at issue is whether assimilation theories about white ethnics using political machines to promote social and economic mobility have much foundation in fact (Parenti, 1970a). It is suggested that what brought about upward mobility for ethnic immigrants was the same thing that assisted everyone else: the New Deal and the improvement in the general standard of living for other white Americans brought about by an expanding economy (Hamilton, 1982; Parenti, 1970a).

Whether assimilation theories are accurate or not, the structures of urban politics did allow political machines controlled by white ethnics to provide jobs, social welfare benefits, and business opportunities primarily if not exclusively to their ethnic constituencies. Eventually these structures were changed by progressive reform movements so that the opportunity to use public power to serve particular constituencies no longer existed when the transition to black rule occurred in the seventies. For example, for Curley's administration in Boston and for the bosses of Tammany Hall, lawsuits to stop preferential hiring of members of the Irish community were never a serious threat. For black mayors, however, from Birmingham to Detroit to Richmond, lawsuits challenging the provision of jobs and city contracts for black citizens are relatively commonplace.

Progressive reform changed not only the structures of urban politics but also the patterns of bias within these structures. The new patterns disadvantaged African-Americans in the political process while they advantaged new groups. The progressive movement introduced new values into the political culture that make it difficult for black administrations to provide substantive as well as symbolic rewards to black constituencies. In addition, reform changed the ways in which poor and unorganized citizens were linked to the polity, resulting in demobilization and depoliticization of the poor in the cities.

Even the basic ethos of the political system changed under reform governments, from a politics of power to one of efficiency (Grimshaw, 1984). Public bureaucracies replaced machines for the distribution of social welfare benefits. Unlike political machines, the bureaucracies were not even symbolically accountable and responsive to their clientele. Unorganized citizens, especially the poor, were no longer linked to the polity through political parties and city hall—a system that, despite its flaws, did provide poor ethnic citizens with some measure of political currency: their vote. Now poor citizens were linked to the polity through bureaucratic agencies, with quasi-governmental power insulated from popular control (Harrigan, 1985). One consequence of this was that by the 1960s and 1970s urban political movements developed among Hispanic and African-American populations who sought popular control of public bureaucracies, that is, community control of schools, welfare agencies, public health-care providers, and the police (Fainstein & Fainstein, 1974).

Progressive reform effectively discredited the private-favoring ethos of "to the victor go the spoils" that dominated political culture during the era of political "machines." In its place a public-regarding ethos evolved, according to which the use of public resources for private gain could only be legitimized in terms of the general public good (Harrigan, 1985). Predominantly upper-class Protestant reformers, supported by other groups, sought to break the power of the predominantly lower-class Catholic political bosses in the name of "good government." Changes in political structure were to put an end to widespread graft and corruption. Historians remind us, however, that whatever else the progressive reform movement did, it did not eliminate corruption from the urban political landscape. Progressive reform may have simply replaced the ethnic political machine with a new kind of machine, one which symbolically served black interests better, but which left black citizens as unrepresented, excluded, and manipulated as before (Fainstein & Fainstein, 1974; Harrigan, 1985). The politics of exclusion has thus worked to the detriment of black political interests in the North and West as well as the South. Even so, disfranchisement in the South became the primary target of efforts to end second-class citizenship in American political life.

The focus of much of the political activity among African-Americans since 1940 has been on getting the right to participate on an equal basis. This is what Hamilton (1986) refers to as a politics of rights. As black political participation increased and the structures of racial politics changed, assessments began to be made of the limits and potential of political activity for addressing social and economic ills (Preston, Henderson, & Puryear, 1982). The politics of rights was supplanted by a politics of resources (Hamilton, 1986). The salient concern shifted from participating in the political system to the terms of that participation and to the likely consequences of that participation.

One of the most important contemporary issues is the degree to which black political activity can lead to improvements in the economic and social status of African-Americans. What are the limits and potential of political participation for achieving black aspirations; what are the strategic and policy implications of contemporary political evolution; and what are the directions and future possibilities for political action? The question

Martin Luther King, Jr., raised in 1968 remains a critical one today: where do we go from here?

It has only been since the late sixties that the third obstacle to the attainment of political influence and effective representation for black citizens—the way in which power is structured—has received some attention. Political violence and political movements in the North and West, where African-Americans had not been excluded from the franchise, brought into sharp relief the necessity for continuing the struggle for political power. The transformation of protest into politics did yield victories in local political contests. But the initial euphoria generated by the capture of city hall eventually gave way to more sober assessments of the limits of public power.

Explanations for the limitations of conventional politics generally focus on the built-in constraints on public policy-making (Hamilton, 1982; Greenberg, Milner, & Olson, 1971; Katznelson & Kesselman, 1987). The ideology of democratic liberalism, it is reasoned, removes certain issues from the legitimate realm of public discussion. Because government is limited in a constitutional system, certain issues are considered "private," and as such are beyond the scope of public decision makers. One of these issues, it is argued, is the use of public political resources to enhance economic position or to stimulate social mobility (Jaynes & Williams, 1989). Not only does such an explanation contradict widely accepted definitions for politics—the authoritative allocation of value (Easton, 1971) or decisions about who gets what, when, and how (Lasswell, 1958)—it also ignores the fact that much contemporary and historical policy-making calls into question this concept of limits (Greenberg, 1986; Harris, 1986; Dolbeare & Edelman, 1981).

A number of examples raise significant questions about the notion that it is unacceptable in our system of government to use politics to enhance economic or allocational status. General policies as well as government largesse given to specific economic actors dramatically contradict assumptions about the limits of political decision making on economic allocation.[7] There has been only minor public outcry about spending between 150 and 200 billion taxpayer dollars to bail out failed savings and loans (S & L) institutions. On the contrary, the S & L bailout, as with other uses of public resources in the private sector, is considered to be a legitimate use of public power to impact private economic activity.

The issue, then, is not *whether* public power should be used to enhance private allocational status, but *for whom*. Therefore, conventional political analysts are not necessarily mistaken when they claim that the conventional limits of politics in our system make it difficult to use politics to alter the allocational status of black Americans. Rather, a broader analytical perspective is required to explain this apparent contradiction. A broader perspective indicates that for some groups in the polity (elites) the use of public power to support economic status is considered legitimate. For other groups (nonelites) the use of public power to support economic status is not considered legitimate, except perhaps in a period of crisis. How are these differential sets of rules justified? And how does the existence of differential rules in the polity impact black political aspirations? These questions direct attention to the third obstacle to the attainment of political power for African-Americans: the way in which power is structured in the United States.

Scholars debate the comparative merits of a number of competing theories and models of American politics (Dye, 1979; Parenti, 1970b, 1983; Greenberg, 1986; Katznelson & Kesselman, 1987; Hawley & Wirt, 1968; Dolbeare & Edelman, 1981; Dahl, 1961; F. Hunter, 1953; Mills, 1956; Connolly, 1967; Mayo, 1960; Polsby, 1963; Lindblom, 1977; Bachrach & Baratz, 1962). This debate is not esoteric in terms of black political interests. A review of this debate indicates that power is organized both privately and publicly in the United States. There are important structures of mediation between the two. Thus, public officials do not simply carry out the formal role expectations of their positions; rather they act as brokers between public policy and private power.

The traditional concept of American politics as a constitutional system with clearly defined constraints on public power and policy-making limits discussion to the arena of public power and politics. The context and limits of the public exercise of power, however, are influenced to varying degrees by the structure and organization of private power. One way this private organization of power influences decision-making is through the power of nondecisions (Bachrach & Baratz, 1962)—that is, the power to set the public agenda. When policymakers and politicians try to move outside the "acceptable" ranges of public life, they encounter enormous resistance and oftentimes defeat of their proposals. Some major aspects of life in the United States, such as the rights of private ownership or the presence and persistence of economic inequality, never receive the attention and debate that they deserve (Domhoff, 1978). Candidates for political office do not build them into their campaigns, nor do elected and appointed officials raise them in legislative chambers. Thus, merely electing black candidates to public office does not ensure that issues of concern to African-Americans, such as economic inequality between racial groups, will receive appropriate attention in the public policy-making process. Any comprehensive reading of black political life in America has to confront the implications of the public/private dimensions of power.

There are inherent limits, then, on the exercise of power within the political system. The fragmentation and dispersal of power and policy-making through federalism, separation of powers, and other constitutional provisions does not invalidate the power elite thesis. The structure of private power may be conceptualized in many ways—as monolithic and hierarchical, as pluralistic, as institutionally based, as oligarchical, as plutocratic—and in all its forms private power influences public decision making. This influence is not normally directly exercised through the state (i.e., national, state, or local governmental structures). Rather, private power is exercised through mediating structures, some examples of which include political parties, political campaigns, lobbying, think tanks, the media, the educational system, policy formulation, and the law.

The contemporary challenge for black politics goes beyond the capture of elective office, participation in conventional political arenas, and placement of concerns of black citizens on public agendas. The larger challenge concerns effective representation of black interests in all the significant arenas of policy formulation: elite and nonelite, public and private. Effective representation[8] requires substantive inclusion of African-Americans in all areas of political life. It is the political inclusion of African-Americans that alone holds out the promise of transforming American politics, of bringing about effective representation for all Americans within the body politic.

Historically, political change has occurred in the United States in evolutionary ways. Changes in political structure were accompanied by changes in the patterns of bias within the system (Harrigan, 1985). These patterns of bias automatically advantage some in the political system while automatically disadvantaging others. There is a need to identify the patterns of bias that operate at various levels of American politics to limit black aspirations. There is also a need to stimulate and legitimize public debate of options for political change that could move us from a politics of exclusion to one of inclusion.

A politics of inclusion is concerned with more than the effective representation of black interests in the political system. For example, the political movements of the sixties generally sought black empowerment in a context of the creation of a just society. The nation was called upon to live up to the highest ideals of the American creed. Indeed, central to Myrdal's thesis of the "American Dilemma" was the contradiction between the espoused ideals and the historical practices of white Americans, especially with regard to issues of race (Myrdal, 1944).

A politics of inclusion resurrects the moral dimension of American politics. The demand for effective representation of all citizens moves us toward the ideal of a just society in the true sense of democracy—one in which political liberty exists because all citizens not only have the right to vote, but also have an equal chance to influence effectively the decisions that affect their lives.

SUMMARY

An evaluation of the participation of African-Americans in the political life of the nation since the 1940s indicates a tremendous upsurge in voter registration and turnout, especially in the aftermath of the passage of the Voting Rights Act of 1965. In presidential elections, the gap narrowed between participation rates of blacks and whites. Increased participation meant that elected officials became more sensitive to black needs when the interests of African-Americans and Euro-Americans converged. However, old problems remain and new issues emerge as the limits of political participation become more evident. These new issues include how to manage ethnic and racial group relations, how to manage interracial conflict, and how to keep black elected officials accountable to their constituencies.

As long as the politics of exclusion is operative in American politics, both conventional and nonconventional alternatives of political participation will be important for African-Americans. Conventional politics continue to be significant not only because of access to public power centers and policy-making, but also because of the brokerage factor as well as the political, educational, and symbolic functions that officeholders carry out in the public and private arenas of power. Concomitantly, nonconventional politics will continue to be an important avenue for mobilizing black political aspirations as long as the politics of exclusion mitigate against effective political participation in the polity.

The political behavior of African-Americans in the period 1940 to the present is best understood as a search for power in both conventional and nonconventional political terms. The goal has been not only to gain full participation in the public political arena, but to achieve effective political representation throughout the polity. The struggle for a politics of inclusion, which focused during the civil rights movement on gaining access to conventional political processes, continues as a search for the ways and means to achieve full participation in all political arenas of the polity.

APPENDIX

A typology of group-polity, group-leadership relationships can be constructed using the three dimensions—descriptive representativeness, responsiveness (substantive representation), and efficacy (actual representation)—yielding eight possible ideal-types:

Typology of Group-Polity Relationship and International Group Structure

	Representative		Not Representative	
	Responsive	Not Responsive	Responsive	Not Responsive
Efficacious	1 Clear democracy	2 Detached oligarchy	5 Paternalism	6 Efficacious autocracy
Not efficacious	3 Ineffectual democracy	4 Apparent democracy	7 Ineffectual paternalism	8 Clear tyranny

1. The policy or the group's leadership is descriptively representative, responsive, and efficacious. We may call this case *clear democracy.*
2. The polity or the group's leadership is descriptively representative and efficacious, but is unresponsive to group needs. Here the forms of democracy are intact and are seen to be operating, but the group's participating leadership elite has been co-opted or bought off so that while it participates in the larger political system, it no longer speaks for those it claims to represent. We may call this case *detached oligarchy.*
3. The polity or the group's leadership is descriptively representative, responsive, but ineffectual. We may call this case *ineffectual democracy.*
4. In this fairly unlikely case, the polity or the group's leadership, though descriptively representative, is both unresponsive and ineffectual. The polity or group leadership's unresponsiveness is masked by its lack of effectiveness. We may, therefore, call this case *apparent democracy.*
5. The polity or the group's leadership is responsive though not descriptively representative, but is efficacious in promoting its goals. We may call this case *paternalism.*

6. The polity or the group's leadership is neither descriptively representative nor responsive, but promotes its goals effectively. We may call this case *efficacious autocracy.*
7. The polity or the group's leadership, though ineffectual and not descriptively representative, does try to be responsive. We may call this case *ineffectual paternalism.*
8. The polity or the group's leadership is not descriptively responsive, nor is it responsive or effectual. We may call this case *clear tyranny.*

Utilizing this typology, we can ask, cross-nationally, if racial group relationships are characterized by high or low descriptive representation, responsiveness, and efficacy; in what combination; and with what consequences.

NOTES

1. Examples include lynchings, nightriders, murders, burnings, mob violence, physical assaults, and economic deprivations, i.e., losing a job, denial of loans, etc.

2. The white primary was the process (legal until 1944) of excluding blacks from the Democratic party and thereby precluding blacks from voting in the Democratic primaries. This was the most effective mechanism used to disfranchise blacks throughout the South.

3. The concepts of "critical" and "routine" are used by Katznelson to define critical and routine periods in the history of racial politics. He writes: "In social terms, the student of race politics can distinguish between critical and routine historical periods, the former being the periods when critical structural political decisions were made institutionalizing power differentials between racial groups. . . . Since 'organization is the mobilization of bias,' . . . [Schattschneider, 1960] structure not only limits but also shapes the direction of choice. With Apter 'the structure may be defined as the relationships in a social situation which limit the choice process to a particular range of alternative,' while 'the behavioral may be defined as the selection process in choice, i.e., deciding between alternatives' . . . [Apter and Eckstein, 1963]. Utilizing this distinction, critical decisions are structural, routine decisions behavioral . . . [McFarland, 1969]" (Katznelson, 1976).

4. This issue is discussed more fully in the last section of this chapter, Political Exclusion, Political Power, and Black Politics.

5. Judge J. F. Dillon, in the 1860s, in what became known as the Dillon rule, established the interpretation of local powers that makes local governments creations that exist at the pleasure of the state. The state can alter their structure or even abolish them (Goodall & Sprengel, 1975, p. 38).

6. Coleman Young was able to have this provision changed; Maynard Jackson was not. Jackson had to wait out the mayoralty of Andrew Young before running again successfully for his third term.

7. Tax abatements, price supports, favorable tax policies aimed at specific industries or corporations, the use of governmental power to negotiate favorable trade policies, and progrowth urban renewal policies are examples of general policies. The use of Urban Development Action Grant monies in Rhode Island to refurbish a hotel lobby, the use of PIC monies to pay a California agribusiness not to plant rice in a lake, and the Chrysler bailout are all examples of transfer payments to specific companies.

8. See Katznelson (1976, pp. 26–28) for a discussion of the meaning of effective and efficacious representation within the context of the structure of racial politics. Also see the Appendix for his typology of group-polity relations and internal group structure.

REFERENCES

Alford, R. R., & Friedland, R. (1975). Political participation and public policy. In A. Inkeles, J. Coleman, and N. Smelser (Eds.), *Annual Review of Sociology, 1*, 429–479. Palo Alto: Annual Reviews.

Altshuler, A. A. (1970). *Community control: The black demand for participation in large American cities.* New York: Pegasus.

Apter, D. E., & Eckstein, J. (1963). *Comparative politics: A reader.* New York: Free Press.

Bachrach, P., & Baratz, M. S. (1962). The two faces of power. *American Political Science Review, 56*, 547–552.

Bachrach, P., & Baratz, M. S. (1970). *Power and poverty.* New York: Oxford University Press.

Baker, R. S. (1964). *Following the color line: American Negro citizenship in the progressive era.* New York: Harper and Row. (Original edition published in 1908.)

Barker, L., & Walters, R. W. (Eds.). (1989). *Jesse Jackson's 1984 presidential campaign: Challenge and change in American politics.* Urbana, IL: University of Illinois Press.

Bass, J., & DeVries, W. (1976). *The transformation of southern politics.* New York: Basic Books.

Bell, D. A. (1980). *Race, racism, and American law* (2nd ed.). Boston: Little Brown.

Black, E. (1976). *Southern governors and civil rights.* Cambridge, MA: Harvard University Press.

Boamah-Wiafe, D. (1990). *The black experience in contemporary America.* Omaha, NE: Wisdom Publications.

Bolce, L. H. (1985). Reagan and the reverse gender gap. *Public Opinion Quarterly, 15*, 372–385.

Bolce, L., & Gray, S. H. (1979). Blacks, whites, and race politics. *Public Interest, 54*, 61–75.

Breitman, G. (1967). *The last year of Malcolm X: The evolution of a revolutionary*. New York: Pathfinder Press.

Brown v. Board of Education, 347 U.S. 483 (1954).

Brown, H. R. (1969). *Die nigger die*. New York: Dial Press.

Bush, R. (Ed.). (1984). *The new black vote*. San Francisco: Synthesis Publications.

Button, J. W. (1978). *Black violence*. Princeton, NJ: Princeton University Press.

Caldwell, E. (1978). The rising status of commitment. *Black Enterprise, 9*, 38–42.

Campbell, D., & Feagin, J. R. (1975). Black politics in the South. *Journal of Politics, 37*, 129–162.

Carmichael, S., & Hamilton, C. V. (1967). *Black power*. New York: Random House.

Carson, C. (1981). *In struggle: SNCC and the black awakening of the 1960s*. Cambridge, MA: Harvard University Press.

Cassel, C. (1979). Changes in electoral participation in the South. *Journal of Politics, 41*, 907–917.

Combs, M., & Comer, J. (1982). Race and capital punishment: A longitudinal analysis. *Phylon, 43*, 350–359.

Connolly, W. (1967). *Political science and ideology*. New York: Atherton Press.

Coombs, D., Alsikafi, M. H., Bryan, C. H., & Webber, I. (1977). Black political control in Greene County, Alabama. *Rural Sociology, 42*, 398–406.

Dahl, R. A. (1961). *Who governs?* New Haven, CT: Yale University Press.

Danigelis, N. (1978). Black political participation in the United States. *American Sociological Review, 43*, 756–771.

Davidson, C. (1984). Minority vote dilution. In C. Davidson (Ed.), *Minority vote dilution*. Washington, DC: Howard University Press.

Davidson, C., & Korbel, G. (1981). At-large elections and minority group representation. *Journal of Politics, 43*, 982–1005.

Dolbeare, K. M., & Edelman, M. J. (1981). *American politics* (4th ed.). Lexington, MA: D. C. Heath.

Domhoff, G. W. (1978). *The powers that be*. New York: Vintage.

Drake, S. C., & Cayton, R. C. (1962). *Black metropolis*. New York: Harper and Row. (Original edition published in 1945)

Dye, T. K. (1979). *Who's running America? The Carter years* (2nd ed.). Englewood Cliffs, NJ: Prentice-Hall.

Easton, D. (1971). *The political system: An inquiry into the state of political science* (2nd ed.). New York: Knopf.

Eisinger, P. K. (1980). *The politics of displacement: Racial and ethnic transition in three American cities*. New York: Academic Press.

Eisinger, P. K. (1983). *Black employment in city government, 1973–1980*. Washington, DC: Joint Center for Political Studies.

Fainstein, N. I., & Fainstein, S. S. (1974). *Urban political movements: The search for power by minority groups in American cities*. Englewood Cliffs, NJ: Prentice-Hall.

Farley, R. (1984). *Blacks and whites*. Cambridge, MA: Harvard University Press.

Feagin, J. R. (1972). Civil rights voting by southern congressmen. *Journal of Politics, 34*, 484–499.

Franklin, J. H. (1967). *From slavery to freedom*. New York: Knopf.

Frazier, E. F. (1939). *The Negro family in the United States*. Chicago: University of Chicago Press.

Frazier, E. F. (1957). *Black bourgeoisie: The rise of a new middle class in the United States*. Glencoe, IL: Free Press.

Georgakas, D., & Surkin, M. (1975). *Detroit: I do mind dying*. New York: St. Martin's Press.

Gilliam, F., & Whitby, K. J. (1987). Race, class and abortion attitudes: An ethclass model. Paper presented at the annual meeting of the Midwest Political Science Association, April, 1987, Chicago, IL.

Glantz, O. (1960). The Negro voter in northern industrial cities. *Western Political Quarterly, 13*, 999–1010.

Gomillion v. Lightfoot, 364 U.S. 399, 110 (1960).

Goodall, L. E., & Sprengel, D. P. (1975). *The American metropolis* (2nd ed.). Columbus, OH: Charles E. Merrill.

Granberg, D., & Granberg, B. (1980). Abortion attitudes, 1965–1980: Trends and determinants. *Family Planning Perspectives, 12*(5), 250–261.

Greeley, A. (1971). *Why can't they be like us?* New York: E. P. Dutton.

Greenberg, E. S. (1986). *The American political system: A radical approach* (4th ed.). Boston: Little Brown.

Greenberg, E. S., Milner, N., & Olson, D. J. (1971). *Black politics: The inevitability of conflict readings*. New York: Holt, Rinehart, and Winston.

Greer, E. S. (1979). *Big steel*. New York: Monthly Review Press.

Grimshaw, W. (1984). Is Chicago ready for reform? Or, a new agenda for Harold Washington. In M. G. Holli and P. M. Green (Eds.), *The making of the mayor: Chicago 1983*. Grand Rapids, MI: Eerdmans.

Hall, E. J., & Ferree, M. M. (1986). Race differences in abortion attitudes. *Public Opinion Quarterly, 50*, 193–207.

Hamilton, C. V. (1982). Foreword. In M. B. Preston, L. J. Henderson, Jr., and P. Puryear (Eds.), *The new black politics: The search for power*. New York: Longman.

Hamilton, C. V. (1986). Social policy and the welfare of black Americans: From rights to resources. *Political Science Quarterly, 101* (2), 239–255.

Harrigan, J. J. (1985). *Political change in the metropolis* (3rd ed.). Boston: Little Brown.

Harris, F. R. (1986). *America's democracy: The ideal and the reality* (3rd ed.). Glenview, IL: Scott, Foresman.

Hawley, W. D., & Wirt, F. M. (Eds.). (1968). *The search for community power.* Englewood Cliffs, NJ: Prentice-Hall.

Herbers, J. (1965, February 2). Dr. King and 770 others seized in Alabama protest. *New York Times*, p. 1.

Holden, M. (1973). *The politics of the black "nation."* New York: Chandler.

Holli, M. G., & Green, P. M. (Eds.). (1984). *The making of the mayor: Chicago 1983.* Grand Rapids, MI: Eerdmans.

Hunter, D. H. (1974). *Federal review of voting changes.* Washington, DC: Joint Center for Political Studies.

Hunter, F. (1953). *Community power structure.* Chapel Hill, NC: University of North Carolina Press.

James, M. (1973). *The people's lawyers.* New York: Holt, Rinehart and Winston.

Jaynes, G. D., & Williams, R. M., Jr. (Eds.). (1989). *A common destiny: Blacks and American society.* Washington, DC: National Academy Press.

Jennings, J. (1990). *The politics of black empowerment: The transformation of black activism in urban America.* Detroit: Wayne State University Press.

Jennings, J., & King, M. (1986). *From access to power: Black politics in Boston.* Cambridge, MA: Schenkman Books.

Johnson, M., & Roark, J. L. (1984). *Black masters: A free family of color in the Old South.* New York: W. W. Norton.

Jones, M. (1972). *Black officeholders in local governments in the South.* Paper presented at the 68th annual meeting of the American Political Science Association, Los Angeles.

Karnig, A., & Welch, S. (1980). *Black representation and urban policy.* Chicago: University of Chicago Press.

Katznelson, I. (1976). *Black men, white cities: Race, politics, and migration in the United States, 1900–30, and Britain, 1948–68.* Chicago: University of Chicago Press.

Katznelson, I. (1981). *City trenches: Urban politics and the patterning of class in the United States* (2nd ed.). Chicago: University of Chicago Press.

Katznelson, I., & Kesselman, M. (1987). *The politics of power: A critical introduction to American government* (3rd ed.). San Diego: Harcourt Brace Jovanovich.

Keech, W. R. (1968). *The impact of Negro voting.* Chicago: Rand McNally.

Kernell, S. (1973). Comment: A re-evaluation of black voting in Mississippi. *American Political Science Review, 67*, 1307–1318.

King, M. L., Jr., (1968). *Where do we go from here? Chaos or community.* Boston: Beacon Press.

Lasswell, H. (1958). *Politics: Who gets what, when, how.* Cleveland: Meridian Books.

Levy, M. R., & Kramer, M. S. (1972). *The ethnic factor.* New York: Simon and Schuster.

Lindblom, C. (1977). *Politics and markets.* New York: Basic Books.

Lipset, S. M. (1963). *Political man: The social bases of politics.* New York: Doubleday.

Lipsky, M. (1980). *Street-level bureaucracy: Dilemmas of the individual in public services.* New York: Russell Sage Foundation.

Marshall, D., & Tabb, D. (1985), *Minority participation and political payoffs in California.* New York: Basic Books.

Mayo, H. (1960). *An introduction to democratic theory.* New York: Oxford University Press.

Mayor LaGuardia's Commission on the Harlem Riot. (1969). *The complete report of Mayor LaGuardia's Commission on the Harlem Riot of March 19, 1935.* New York: Arno Press.

McAdam, D. (1982). *Political process and the development of black insurgency.* Chicago: University of Chicago Press.

McAdam, D. (1988). *Freedom summer.* New York: Oxford University Press.

McBride, D., & Little, M. (1981). The Afro-American elite, 1930–1940. *Phylon, 42*, 105–119.

McClean, V. (1984). Historical examples of black conservatism. *Western Journal of Black Studies, 8*, 148–153.

McFarland, A. (1969). *Power and leadership in pluralist systems.* Stanford, CA: Stanford University Press.

Meier, A. (Ed.). (1970). *The transformation of activism.* Chicago: Aldine Publishing.

Milbrath, L., & Goel, M. (1977). *Political participation* (2nd ed.). Chicago: Rand McNally.

Miller, W. E., Miller, A. H., & Scheider, E. J. (1980). *American National Election Studies data sourcebook, 1952–1978.* Cambridge, MA: Harvard University Press.

Mills, C. W. (1956). *The power elite.* New York: Oxford University Press.

Miroff, B. (1979). *Pragmatic illusions: The presidential politics of John F. Kennedy.* New York: Longman.

Morris, A. (1984). *The origins of the civil rights movements: Black communities organizing for change.* New York: Free Press.

Moss, L. E. (1977). *Black political ascendancy in urban centers and black control of the local police function: An exploratory analysis.* San Francisco: R & E Associates.

Moynihan, D. P. (1972). The schism in black America. *Public Interest, 27*, 3–24.

Myrdal, G. (1944). *An American dilemma: The Negro problem and modern democracy.* New York: Harper and Row.

Neiburg, H. L. (1969). *Political violence.* New York: St. Martin's Press.

Olsen, M. (1970). Social and political participation of blacks. *American Sociological Review, 35*, 682–697.

Parent, W., & Stekler, P. (1985). The political implications of economic stratification in the black community. *Western Political Quarterly, 38*, 521–537.

Parenti, M. (1970a). Assimilation and counter-assimilation: From civil rights to black radicalism. In P. Green and S. Levison (Eds.), *Power and community: Dissenting essays in political science*. New York: Vintage.

Parenti, M. (1970b). Power and pluralism: A view from the bottom. *Journal of Politics*, *32*, 501–530.

Parenti, M. (1983). *Democracy for the few* (4th ed.). New York: St. Martin's Press.

Parker, F. R. (1984). Racial gerrymandering and legislative reapportionment. In C. Davidson (Ed.), *Minority vote dilution*. Washington, DC: Howard University Press.

Pettigrew, T. (1964). *A profile of the Negro American*. Princeton, NJ: D. Van Nostrand.

Piven, F. F., & Cloward, R. A. (1977). *Poor people's movements*. New York: Vintage.

Polsby, N. (1963). *Community power and political theory*. New Haven: Yale University Press.

Preston, M. B., Henderson, L. J., Jr., & Puryear, P. (Eds.). (1982). *The new black politics: The search for political power*. New York: Longman.

Raines, H. (1983). *My soul is rested: Movement days in the Deep South remembered*. New York: Penguin Books. Reprint.

Ransford, H. E., & Miller, J. (1983). Race, sex and feminist outlooks. *American Sociological Review*, *48*, 45–59.

Reed, A. L., Jr. (1986). *The Jesse Jackson phenomenon*. New Haven: Yale University Press.

Salaman, L. M., & Van Evera, S. (1973). Fear, apathy, and discrimination. *American Political Science Review*, *67*, 1288–1306.

Schattschneider, E. E. (1960). *The semisovereign people: A realist's view of democracy in America*. Hinsdale, IL: Dryden Press.

Sears, D. O., & McConahay, J. B. (1973). *The politics of violence: The new urban blacks and the Watts riot*. Boston: Houghton Mifflin.

Secret, P., Johnson, J., & Welch,. S. (1986). Racial differences in attitudes toward school prayer. *Social Science Quarterly*, *67*, 877–886.

Seltzer, R., & Smith, R. (1985). Race and ideology: A research note measuring liberalism and conservatism in black America. *Phylon*, *46*, 98–105.

Sherman, A. K., & Kolker, A. (1987). *The social basis of politics*. Belmont, CA: Wadsworth.

Sigelman, L., & Welch, S. (1984). Race, gender, and opinion towards black and female presidential candidates. *Public Opinion Quarterly*, *48*(2), 467–475.

Simpson, G. E., & Yinger, J. M. (1985). *Racial and cultural minorities* (5th ed.). New York: Plenum Press.

Sites, P., & Mullins, E. (1985). The American black elite: 1930–1978. *Phylon*, *46*, 269–280.

Smith v. Allwright 321 U.S. 649 (1944).

Thompson, D. C. (1974). *Sociology of the black experience.* Westport, CT: Greenwood Press.

U.S. Commission on Civil Rights. (1959). *Report.* Washington, DC: U.S. Government Printing Office.

U.S. Commission on Civil Rights. (1961). *Report: Book 1, voting.* Washington, DC: U.S. Government Printing Office

U.S. Commission on Civil Rights. (1968). *Political participation.* Washington, DC: U.S. Government Printing Office.

U.S. Commission on Civil Rights. (1975). *The Voting Rights Act: Ten years after.* Washington, DC: U.S. Government Printing Office.

U.S. Commission on Civil Rights. (1982). *Confronting racial isolation in Miami.* Washington, DC: U.S. Government Printing Office.

U.S. Kerner Commission. (1968). *The report of the National Advisory Commission on Civil Disorders.* Washington, DC: U.S. Government Printing Office.

Verba, S., & Nie, N. H. (1972). *Participation in America.* New York: Harper and Row.

Voter Education Project. (1976). *Election law changes in cities and counties in Georgia.* Atlanta: Author.

Walton, H., Jr. (1985). *Invisible politics.* Albany, NY: State University of New York Press.

Welch, S., & Combs, M. (1983). Interracial differences in opinion on public issues in the 1970s. *Western Journal of Black Studies, 7,* 136–141.

Welch, S., & Combs, M. (1985). Intra-racial differences in attitudes of blacks: Class cleavages or consensus? *Phylon, 46,* 91–97.

Welch, S., & Foster, L. (1987, October). Class and conservatism in the black community. *American Politics Quarterly.*

Widick, B. J. (1972). *Detroit: City of race and class violence.* Chicago: Quadrangle Books.

Williams, L. (1987). Black political progress in the 1980s: The electoral arenas. In M. B. Preston, L. Henderson, and P. Puryear (Eds.), *The new black politics: The search for political power* (2nd ed.). New York: Longman.

Wolfinger, R. E., & Rosenstone, S. J. (1980). *Who votes?* New Haven: Yale University Press.

Zinn, H. (1964). *SNCC: The new abolitionists.* Boston: Beacon Press.

Zipp, J. F. (1985). Perceived representativeness and voting. *American Political Science Review, 79,* 50–61.

4

The Administration of Justice

Wornie L. Reed, with Roy Austin, Obie Clayton, Nolan Jones, Barry A. Krisberg, Hubert G. Locke, Alphonso Pinkney, Michael L. Radelet, and Susan Welch

If the Russian novelist Fyodor Dostoyevsky is correct that "the degree of civilization in a society can be judged by entering its prisons" (Worton, 1977), what one finds in correctional institutions in the United States does not speak well of civilized impulses in American society. This is particularly true with respect to the nation's African-American populace whose numbers in prison populations are immensely disproportionate to the percentage of African-Americans in the general U.S. population or to even the most liberal estimates of black criminal offenders. A look at the issue of African-Americans in relation to the corrections system in particular, and the criminal justice system in general, therefore, is one way of examining the broader question of the status of African-Americans in American society itself.

The facts, broadly stated, are as follows: African-Americans, together with smaller percentages of Hispanics and members of other racial minorities, currently constitute the majority of American prisoners (Garwood, 1992). In 1987, African-Americans accounted for approximately 12% of the United States population and 47% of the prison population (Garwood, 1992). This high proportion of blacks among American prisoners levelled off in the 1970s after increasing substantially in the 1950s and 1960s—from 29% in 1949 to 38% in 1960 to 48% in 1974 (Horton & Smith, 1990).

Between 1940 and 1949 61% of prisoners executed were black. This was a substantial increase over the previous decade, 1930–1939, when 49% of persons executed were black. The percentage decreased to 52% between 1950 and 1959 and 49% between 1960 and 1967; and it decreased to 35% in the period 1977–1987 (Horton & Smith, 1990). However, the percentage of persons receiving a death sentence is increasing as currently over 40% of all persons awaiting execution are black (Greenfield, 1992). Black prisoners under death sentence for capital offenses represent over 40% of all persons awaiting execution (Greenfield, 1992). Perhaps most alarming of all, black offenders represent the highest percentages in prison populations in those states where the percentage of black citizens in the general state population is disproportionately low (Institute for Public Policy and Management, 1986).

The scholarly literature is voluminous, controversial, and inconclusive as to why such gross disparities occur. Arguments range from "a pattern of apparent racial discrimination" (Christianson, 1980) to the view that minorities are more likely to be imprisoned because they commit a disproportionate share of serious and violent crimes (Blumstein, 1982). Midway between these two positions lies the stance that while minorities may commit a larger share of serious and violent crimes, the legal system may compound matters by treating African-American offenders differently than their white counterparts (Petersilia, 1983). Only the first argument would begin to explain the paradox of the highest rates of incarceration of black offenders being found in states where the percentage of black residents is the lowest.

The corrections system is only one facet—the institutional end point—of a complex and intricate process euphemistically termed "the administration of justice" in America. Immense problems that raise questions of race and ethnicity are also found in the other institutional segments of the process: law enforcement, the office of the prosecutor, and the courts. At each stage the issue of equality and fairness with respect to the nation's black citizenry looms large. The following discussion, however, is limited to a set of selected issues: sentencing; capital punishment; juvenile justice; and issues concerning crime, drugs, and race.

SENTENCING

The process by which those accused of crime are handled within the criminal justice process is a complex one. Here we will focus on the treatment, in terms of the determination of sentences, of those convicted. Note, importantly, that this focus largely ignores factors such as the incidence of crime, the treatment of suspects by police in arrests, the decisions of prosecutors to file or dismiss charges, the pretrial treatment of defendants (in obtaining bail or pretrial diversion and thus release, for example), and the decision to convict. At each of these stages, race may be a significant factor.

Even with these caveats in mind, it is important to recognize that sentencing remains a significant part of the criminal justice process. It is at this stage that convicted defendants are put on probation, given a fine or work assignment and allowed to go back to continue their normal activities, or incarcerated and thus separated from the rest of society.

The major question before us here is whether blacks are discriminated against in sentencing decisions. For our purposes, *discriminated against* means that other things being equal, black defendants are given more severe sentences than whites. *Other things* include legal considerations such as the nature and severity of the crime committed and the prior criminal record of the defendant. They may also include extralegal factors such as whether the defendant has received bail or not and whether he or she is being defended by a private or public attorney.

Of course, if police discriminate against blacks in arrests and prosecutors do so in deciding whether to drop charges, then the nature of the prior criminal record, an important predictor of sentencing, will be biased and any analysis of sentencing will be as well. Likewise, if those who are out on bail are less likely to get heavy sentences than those not out on bail, and whites disproportionately receive bail, this too could mean that sentencing research is biased.

Criminal justice researchers have done far more research on discrimination in sentencing than on discrimination at other states of the criminal justice process. The research that has been conducted in other areas has tended to find little discrimination in conviction (cf. Welch, Spohn, and Gruhl, 1984, 1985; Gruhl, Welch, and Spohn, 1984), discrimination on the basis of wealth in setting bail (Lizotte, 1978; LaFree, 1985; Albonetti, 1985), and racial discrimination in the decision to reject charges (Spohn, Welch, & Gruhl, 1981) but not in dismissal once charges are filed.

From the volumes of research that have been done on racial discrepancies in sentencing, the major generalization one can make is that black males are clearly discriminated against in some jurisdictions, but not in others. Evidence of discrimination is most often found in the South, but not exclusively so. Moreover, the question of whether black females are discriminated against has not been extensively examined, although the existing findings indicate little discrimination against them. Thus, it is important in any evaluation of racial disparities in sentencing to examine men and women separately.

Sentencing decisions in criminal cases are made almost entirely by local and state courts. Thus, there is tremendous variation throughout the United States. Findings from one geographic area cannot be generalized to other areas. Indeed, it is quite clear that the amount of racial discrimination in sentencing varies widely across the nation, though not enough localities have been studied to trace much more than crude patterns of this discrimination.

Let us look at the evidence of racial differences in sentencing more carefully.

Problems in Sentencing Research

Observers have noted that black criminal defendants tend to receive more severe sentences than white defendants. Some suggest that this is a result of racial discrimination, while others emphasize wealth discrimination resulting from the inability of poor defendants to obtain private attorneys or pretrial release. This scenario, of course, would disproportionately affect blacks, since they are more likely than whites to be poor. Still others suggest that the more severe sentences of blacks are due to the effect of legal factors, such as prior criminal record or the type of crime committed.

Early studies usually concluded that the disparity in sentencing between blacks and whites was due to racial discrimination (see a review by Hagan, 1974). Most such studies, however, were found by Hagan to have employed inadequate controls or improper statistical techniques. More recent studies (reviews are found in Kleck, 1981; Hagan & Bumiller, 1983; Spohn, Welch, & Gruhl, 1981; Zatz, 1984) have sometimes concluded that the continued disparity in sentencing is indeed due to racial discrimination (Pope, 1975; Levin, 1977; Uhlman, 1977; Sutton, 1978a; Unnever, Frazier, & Heneretta, 1980), while others have focused on wealth discrimination (Lizotte, 1978). More often, however, studies have concluded that the disparity is due to the effect of legal factors (Baab & Furgeson, 1967; Engle, 1971; Cook, 1973; Burke & Turk, 1975; Chiricos & Waldo, 1975; Tiffany, Avichal, & Peters, 1975; Clarke & Koch, 1976; Eisenstein & Jacob, 1977; Lotz & Hewitt, 1977; Gibson, 1978; Sutton, 1978b).

While these more recent studies have corrected for some of the most serious methodological defects of the earlier research, many still have flaws that to some degree account for their different outcomes. Some used a very small number of cases (Clarke & Koch, 1976; Bernstein, Kick, Leung, & Schultz, 1977; Unnever, Frazier, & Heneretta, 1980) or lumped different jurisdictions together (Tiffany et al., 1975; Sutton, 1978a, 1978b; Pope, 1975). this latter occurrence is particularly troublesome because, as we have already noted, different degrees of racial discrimination are manifest in different jurisdictions. Studies using the same appropriate methods and measures for one locality could reach diametrically different conclusions in another locality for the simple reason that the two localities differ in racial discrimination practices.

Other studies included both men and women defendants, but did not provide adequate controls for gender (Unnever et al., 1980). This invalidates findings since men and women defendants tend to be treated differently.

Still other studies used only a small number of offenses, also making generalizations difficult (Cook, 1973; Tiffany, Avichal, & Peters, 1975; Clarke & Koch, 1976). No particular offenses are so typical that just one or a few can be analyzed to discover a pattern of discrimination across all crimes.

Many studies inadequately controlled for relevant legal and extralegal factors, such as seriousness of the charge (Baab & Furgeson, 1967; Burke & Turk, 1975; Pope, 1975; Gibson, 1978; Sigler & Horn, 1986), prior criminal record (Uhlman, 1977), or type of attorney or pretrial bail status (Pope, 1975; Levin, 1977; Gibson, 1978; Sigler & Horn, 1986).

Other studies examined only one sentence decision, even though the sentence is a product of two decisions—the decision whether to incarcerate and the decision on length of sentence. These are separate decisions based upon different criteria; the existence or seriousness of any prior criminal record is the best predictor of the decision to incarcerate, while the seriousness of the charge is the best predictor of length of sentence (Sutton, 1978a). Lumping them together in one measure, or generalizing from one to the other, is misleading and can obscure discrimination.

Finally, the use of inadequate statistical techniques is less common than it used to be, but still exists. Some researchers, for instance, did not use adequate statistical tests of significance techniques (Greenwood et al., 1973; Chiricos & Waldo, 1975; Clarke & Koch, 1976; Levin, 1977; Sigler & Horn, 1986).

Some Findings from Recent Studies That Avoid These Problems

If we examine findings from several recent studies that avoid most of these problems, four major conclusions appear valid.

1. In some communities, but not others, black males are more likely than white males to be sentenced to prison. For example, in one large northern community, black males were more likely than white males to receive prison terms, though they did not differ in overall sentence severity—a measure evaluating the sentence from small fines on one end of the scale to life imprisonment on the other. This discrepancy indicates

the importance of looking at the two aspects of the sentence. The black and white defendants also differed in terms of legal and extralegal factors. Blacks had more serious criminal records and were charged with more serious crimes. They were also more likely than whites to be represented by a public defender, to engage in plea bargaining, to have a high bail set, and to be detained prior to trial (Spohn, Welch, & Gruhl, 1981). A California study (Petersilia, 1983) also found that black defendants were more likely than whites to be incarcerated.

In the California study, blacks were also sentenced to longer terms than whites. In the northern city study, in borderline cases, the judges selected the probation option for whites more often than for blacks and the prison option for blacks more often than for whites. Within each group (incarcerated and not incarcerated) blacks received lighter sentences, thus explaining why there was no difference in the overall sentence severity measure.

Other studies, however, illustrate the variability of discrimination. In Los Angeles, black men were incarcerated at the same rate as white men (Gruhl, Welch, & Spohn, 1984). And, using the same measures and methodology in analyzing six U.S. cities, researchers found no evidence of racial discrimination in sentencing in three southern cities in which black males were more likely to be incarcerated than white males (Welch et al., 1985). In one southern city, black males also received harsher sentences overall. An examination of the plea bargaining process in the three cities where blacks were more likely to go to prison suggested that blacks are less likely to plead guilty. For all defendants, black and white, guilty pleas were associated with lighter sentences, indicating plea bargaining. Yet, blacks received similar sentences to whites when they pled not guilty and went to trial; they were more likely than whites to be incarcerated when they pled guilty. This suggests the existence of more discrimination in the less formal plea bargaining process than in the more formal and open trial process, which is governed tightly by legal rules and procedures.

The finding that blacks are less likely to plead guilty is consistent with findings from other locales (LaFree, 1980; Petersilia, 1983) where the same questions were researched.

2. Other things being equal, female defendants are typically treated less severely than males. They are more likely to have charges dismissed and less likely to be incarcerated (Baab & Furgeson, 1967; Gruhl, Welch, & Spohn, 1984; Spohn, Welch, & Gruhl, 1981). Black women appear to be no exception to this generalization. In studies in Los Angeles and in a large northern city, black women were significantly less likely to be incarcerated than black men (Spohn, Welch, & Gruhl, 1981; Gruhl, Welch, & Spohn,

1984). In Los Angeles black women were treated identically with white women in terms of dismissal of charges, pleas of guilty, and rates of incarceration (Gruhl, Welch, & Spohn, 1984). In the northern city, black women also appeared to be treated similarly to white women, but the sample of white women was too small to draw any firm conclusions (Spohn, Welch, & Gruhl, 1981).

3. The race of the victim is increasingly thought to be important in understanding the process of discrimination in sentencing. This has been obvious in capital punishment cases. It also appears that in at least some kinds of noncapital cases, punishments are most harsh when the offender is black and the victim is white (LaFree, 1980; Myers, 1979).

4. It appears that there is less discrimination in the most formal parts of the criminal justice process, including the decisions to convict, to dismiss charges, and even to sentence, than in the less formal, less open processes, such as the decision to press or reject a charge, the plea bargaining process, the decision made regarding pretrial release, and the arrest itself. Discrimination that enters into the pretrial stages may often be a function of socioeconomic status (cf. discussion in Zatz, 1984).

Despite the large amount of research done on racial discrimination in the criminal justice process, much of which is quite good, it is difficult to generalize widely both because of the variability in racial discrimination among local justice systems and because of the variability in discretion, and hence the possibility for discrimination, in different stages of the process. We know far more about discrimination at the conviction and sentencing stages than at the pretrial stage. It is at the pretrial stage, then, that much more research needs to be done.

CAPITAL PUNISHMENT

Whether it be through lynching or legally imposed capital punishment, the threat or use of death as a punishment has been a powerful means of race intimidation throughout American history. In the nineteenth century, statutes that explicitly considered race were not uncommon. In Virginia, for example, the statutes on the books 150 years ago listed 5 capital crimes for whites but 70 for black slaves (Bowers, 1984, p. 10). Today, historians interested in capital punishment use records of state compensations to slave owners to learn how many slaves were executed.

The federal government's statistics on executions date from the 1930s. Between 1930 and 1967, 3,859 prisoners were executed in the United States, 54% of whom were black. A total of 455 of those executions were for rape, and 405 of the defendants (89%) were black (Wolfgang & Reidel,

1977). There are no known cases in American history in which a white man was executed for the rape of a black woman (Radelet, 1989).

Between 1967 and 1972 no executions were carried out in the United States because of an informal moratorium on executions as states reexamined the issue of capital punishment (U. S. Department of Justice, 1980, p. 1). In 1972 the United States Supreme Court ruled that the death penalty, as then imposed, violated the Constitution (*Furman v. Georgia*, 1972). In this case the Court ruled that the imposition of capital punishment in the cases before it violated the Constitution because of arbitrary and discriminatory application. In his concurring opinion, Justice Brennan noted:

> It also is evident that the burden of capital punishment falls upon the poor, the ignorant, and the underprivileged members of minority groups who are least able to voice their complaints against capital punishment. Their impotence leaves them victims of a sanction which wealthier, better-represented, just-as-guilty persons can escape. So long as the capital sanction is used only against the forlorn, easily forgotten members of society, legislators are content to maintain the status quo, because change would draw attention to the problem and concern might develop. (*Furman v. Georgia*, 1972, Justice Brennan concurring)

In another concurring opinion in the *Furman* case, Justice Marshall wrote: "In recognizing the humanity of our fellow beings, we pay ourselves the highest tribute. We . . . join the approximately 70 other jurisdictions in the world which celebrate their regard for civilization and humanity by shunning capital punishment" (*Furman v. Georgia*, 1972, Justice Marshall concurring).

Significantly, in the *Furman* ruling, the Court did not rule that capital punishment constituted "cruel and unusual punishment"—as prohibited by the Eighth Amendment to the Constitution—but rather, it held that its arbitrary usage was unconstitutional. Because *Furman* invalidated all existing death penalty statutes, many observers thought the Court's decision meant a permanent ban on the death sentence. However, several states interpreted the ruling to imply that a state could reinstitute capital punishment if it could rewrite its death penalty statute to minimize or eliminate arbitrary applications of capital punishment.

In 1976 the Supreme Court agreed to hear five cases on the issue of capital punishment (*Gregg*, *Jurek*, *Profitt*, *Roberts*, *Woodson*). The *Greg*, *Jurek,* and *Profitt* cases came from states that had adopted guided discretion laws for capital cases, while the other two (*Roberts* and *Woodson*) involved challenges to the constitutionality of mandatory death penalty codes. The Court upheld the guided discretion cases in Florida, Georgia, and Texas, but ruled that the mandatory death penalty cases in North Carolina and Louisiana were unconstitutional. The court ruled that if a jurisdiction had capital punishment it could not be mandatory. Mitigating circumstances, the court ruled, must be taken into account, and the prior record of a defendant must be considered as well. Most importantly, though, the court held that capital punishment was constitutional.

Between 1972 and mid-1992, 36 states and the federal government successfully reinstituted death penalty statutes. Between 1977 and mid-1992, 179 inmates were executed, and by June 30, 1992, some 2,572 men and 44 women were under sentences of death, including 1,026 blacks (NAACP Legal Defense Fund, 1992).

The most significant (indeed, the only) progress made in the last 20 years in reducing racial disparities in executions was a 1977 Supreme Court decision that outlawed the death penalty for those convicted of rape (*Coker v. Georgia*, 1977). If we examine only executions for murder, we learn that between 1930 and 1967, 50.1% of these executions involved nonwhites. By mid-1992, 49.81% of those on death row, all of whom stand convicted of murder, are nonwhite. Thus, efforts during the past 15 years to revise death penalty statutes to make them more fair have reduced the relevant minority population by less than one percent.

The death penalty remains a southern phenomenon. Since 1977 over 90% of American executions were conducted in the former states of the Confederacy. Most of the exceptions to this pattern were "consensual" executions, where the inmate dropped his appeals. Since 1977, each of the 11 states of the former Confederacy have executed at least four inmates.

Research that examined the question of racial bias in the application of the death penalty before the 1972 *Furman* decision was both plentiful and alarming in its exposure of racial bias, yet methodologically limited (Kleck, 1981; see Radelet & Vandiver, 1986, for review). Research examining the application of the death sentence since 1972 has found that while sentencing is still correlated with race of defendant, the race of the victim exerts the strongest predictive power. While some of this research has exposed racial bias in the presentencing decisions made by prosecutors (e.g., Radelet & Pierce, 1985; Paternoster, 1984), the bulk of the research has focused on sentencing disparities.

The first such study examined over 16,000 homicide cases in Florida, Georgia, Texas, and Ohio (Bowers & Pierce, 1980). Results indicated that, even when controlling for whether or not the homicide involved an accompanying felony, black defendants convicted of killing whites were more likely to receive the death penalty than were defendants in any of the other three racial configurations (blacks convicted of killing blacks, whites killing whites, or whites killing blacks). Radelet (1981), in a study of Florida homicides that occurred between strangers, found similar patterns as did Jacoby and Paternoster (1982) in South Carolina. In a more comprehensive study, Gross and Mauro (1984) used the FBI's Supplemental Homicide Reports to examine sentencing patterns in eight states (Arkansas, Florida, Georgia, Illinois, Mississippi, North Carolina, Oklahoma, and Virginia). Even when the data were adjusted for the possible influences of whether or not felony circumstances were present, the defendant-victim relationship, and so on, the racial disparities remained.

A simple observation further illustrates the problem. In Florida, between 1972, when its current death penalty statute was passed, and 1987, about 45% of the murder victims were black. Yet of the 400 defendants sentenced to death during this period, only 10% had black victims (Radelet, 1985; Radelet & Mello, 1986).

Opponents of capital punishment had expected that capital punishment would be abolished when another case, *McCleskey v. Kemp* (1987), reached the Supreme Court. In this case, a petition was filed by the NAACP Legal Defense and Educational Fund, Inc., for the defendant, in which 18 claims were raised, one of which maintained that the Georgia capital punishment law was administered in a discriminatory manner in violation of the Eighth and Fourteenth Amendments to the Constitution. The petition was supported by a massive statistical study (Baldus, Woodworth, & Pulaski, 1985, 1990; Baldus, Pulaski, & Woodworth, 1986), which demonstrated that a disparity existed in the imposition of the death sentence in Georgia based on race.

The work of Baldus and his colleagues has been widely hailed as the most sophisticated, detailed, and meticulous study ever conducted on sentencing patterns in the United States. The study examined over 2,000 Georgia murders that occurred from 1973 through 1979. Statewide, defendants charged with killing whites were sentenced to death in 11% of the cases, whereas those charged with killing blacks were condemned in only 1% of the cases. The defendant's race also exerted significant effects on sentencing, but was not as strongly related as was the race of the victim. In trying to explain this association, data were collected on some 230 additional variables that might be hypothesized as affecting sentencing, such as a defendant's prior record as well as other variables. However, even when the effects of these variables were controlled, those charged with killing whites were still 4.3 times more likely to be sentenced to death than were defendants charged with killing blacks. Overall, Baldus and his colleagues concluded that almost one-third of the death sentences imposed in Georgia may be the result of race-of-victim discrimination.

On April 22, 1987, the Supreme Court ruled, in *McCleskey v. Kemp*, that,

> At most, the Baldus study indicates a discrepancy that appears to correlate with race. Apparent disparities in sentencing are an inevitable part of our criminal justice system. . . . Where the discretion that is fundamental to our criminal justice system is involved, we decline to assume that what is unexplained is invidious. (*McCleskey v. Kemp*, 1987)

In its 5–4 decision the Court thus held that a discriminatory result is not necessarily racist and is therefore constitutional. Chief among the dissenters was Justice Brennan, who wrote:

> Warren McClesky's evidence confronts us with the subtle and persistent influence of the past. His message is a disturbing one to a society that has formally repudiated racism, and a frustrating one to a Nation accustomed to regarding its destiny as the product of its own will. Nonetheless, we ignore him at our peril, for we remain imprisoned by the past as long as we deny its influence in the present. (*McCleskey v. Kemp*, 1987)

Brennan continued:

> It is tempting to pretend that minorities on death row share a fate in no way connected to our own, that our treatment of them sounds no echoes beyond the chambers in which they die. Such an illusion is ultimately corrosive, for the reverberations of injustice are not so easily confined . . . and the way in which we choose those who will die reveals the depth of our moral commitment among the living.

The Court's ruling brought forth many indignant responses. The *New York Times* (April 24, 1987), for example, in an editorial entitled "Discrimination in Death? Yes, 5–4," commented: "Death *is* different, and given the chances of grisly error, wrong. But even people who favor capital punishment should cringe as long as death means discrimination." A *New York Times* columnist wrote, "And if 'discrepancies' are inevitable in criminal justice sentencing procedures, is not that in itself an argument against capital punishment? An execution, after all, cannot be undone, no matter if, the day after the switch is pulled or the gas pellets dropped, a 'discrepancy' in the sentencing procedure is proved" (Wicker, 1987, p. 31).

Table 4.1
Race of Victims by Executed Defendants: United States, 1977 to mid-1992

	Race of Defendant					
Race of Victim	White	Black	Hispanic	Asian	Native American	Totals
White	132 (56.9%)	56 (24.1%)	6 (2.6%)	0	1 (0.4%)	195 (84.0%)
Black	1 (0.4)	28 (12.1)	0	0	0	29 (12.5)
Hispanic	0	1 (0.4)	4 (1.7)	0	0	5 (2.1)
Asian	0	2 (0.9)	1 (0.4)	0	0	3 (1.3)
Native American	0	0	0	0	0	0
Totals	133 (57.3%)	87 (37.5%)	11 (4.7%)		1 (0.4%)	232 (99.9%)

Source: NAACP Legal Defense Fund (1992, Summer). Death Row, U.S.A.

Note: A total of 199 persons were executed for a total of 232 murders as some defendants had multiple victims. Percentages do not total 100 because of rounding.

Another syndicated columnist wrote of the progress the United States has made in eradicating sanctioned racism. "That record is what makes the Supreme Court's recent decision on race and capital punishment so distressing. Confronted with powerful evidence that racial feelings play a large part in determining who will live and who will die, the Court chose to close its eyes. It effectively condoned the expression of racism in a profound aspect of our law." He continues, "The reasoning was so unrelated to the facts, so unconvincing, that the opinion sometimes seemed cynical. For an individual to prove that racial feelings figured in his sentence would be almost impossible" (Lewis, 1987, p. A31).

A review of the 179 executions carried out in the United States between 1977 and mid-1992 demonstrates the continuous racial bias in capital punishment cases (see Table 4.1). Although nearly one-half of all murder victims are black (Reed, 1991), less than 13% of all executions during 1977–1989 were the result of the murders of blacks (Table 4.1); and all of these executed defendants were blacks. On the other hand, 84% of executions were for white murders. These great differentials underscore the adverse treatment of African-Americans by the criminal justice system.

THE JUVENILE JUSTICE SYSTEM

Ever-increasing numbers of African-American youth are encountering the criminal justice system, many through first involvement with the juvenile justice system. In the following we will review the nature of differential treatment of African-American youth by this "entry point" to the criminal justice system.

Minority youth are vastly overrepresented in public juvenile correctional facilities in the United States. African-American, Hispanic, and Native American youngsters are incarcerated at a far greater proportion to their representation in the general youth population than are white youth. Minority juvenile incarceration rates are three to four times that for whites. Data on juvenile crime, while revealing a heavy minority involvement in violent crime, cannot alone explain the enormously higher rates of minority incarceration.

Incarceration

In 1982 there were 5,035 more minority youth in public correctional facilities in the United States than there were in 1977—an increase of 26%. Black youngsters accounted for nearly two-thirds of the increase. During this same period, the number of white youth in public facilities declined by 1,765—a drop of 7%. The rise in black juvenile incarceration was particularly large between 1979 and 1982 when most jurisdictions adopted a "get tough" policy toward youth crime and substantially increased juvenile court penalties. It is also clear from the available data that earlier policies designed to remove minor offenders and status offenders from secure confinement benefitted mostly white youngsters (Krisberg et al., 1987).

This racial disparity has continued since 1982. Between 1983 and 1989 the number of black youth in public custody increased by nearly a third (32.2%), while the number of white youth decreased by one-fourth (25.2%) (Garwood, 1992). In 1979 57.4% of all youth in public custody were white. By 1989 whites were only 43.7% of all youth in public custody.

Minority youth are more likely to be confined in higher security facilities and in publicly operated facilities. In 1982, slightly more than half (54%) of the incarcerated white youth were housed in public correctional facilities, whereas 71% of incarcerated black youth and 74% of incarcerated Hispanic youth were confined in public facilities. By 1989 less than half (49.1%) of white youth were in public custody (Garwood, 1992). We know very little about the processes that lead to these results.

The courts may, for example, use private placements for cases they perceive as less threatening to public safety, or private facilities may utilize intake screening criteria that inadvertently reduce the placement of minority youth. Another possible explanation may involve the relative costs of private versus public placements. There is a great need to examine this issue more closely and to identify corrective policy changes.

Some commentators have asserted that the high rates of minority incarceration are a result of the higher numbers of youth in minority communities. We know that over the past two or three decades birthrates among blacks have remained high in comparison to the white birthrates. But these demographic trends are insufficient to account for the large disparities in *rates* of incarceration. For example, in 1982 black males had an incarceration rate of 810 per 100,000 as compared to 183 for white males. Hispanic males had an incarceration rate of 481 per 100,000. Young black females had an incarceration rate of 98 per 100,000 compared to 38 and 40 for white and Hispanic females, respectively. Even more troubling than these statistics is the fact that rates of minority incarceration are growing at a much faster pace than the confinement of white youth.

Minority Youth Involvement in Serious and Violent Youth Crime

Data on minority youth crime are ambiguous and contradictory. For example, data available from the Federal Bureau of Investigation (FBI) show very high rates of minority involvement in serious and violent youth crime. However, the overrepresentation of minorities in arrest statistics does not correlate to the even larger overrepresentation of minorities in incarceration statistics. Further, the FBI arrest data is based only on those who are officially taken into custody; thus, these data may be subject to the differential use of diversion programs or informal release policies.

Recent research from the University of Colorado suggests that arrest statistics may overestimate the extent of minority involvement in serious youth crime (Huizinga & Elliott, 1987). Using responses to a self-report questionnaire administered to a large sample of American teenagers, Huizinga and Elliott found that while black youth reported a slightly higher involvement in serious youth crime, the black-white differences were not nearly large enough to explain the high minority incarceration rates. Moreover, Huizinga and Elliott report that, given equal levels of self-reported crime, black youth were much more likely to be arrested and charged with more serious crimes than their white counterparts. The observations of the University of Colorado researchers are consistent with a long series of studies that have compared self-reported criminal behavior with official arrest statistics (Gold & Reimer, 1975; Bachman, O'Malley, & Johnston, 1978; Petersilia, 1983).

Juvenile Courts

Inherent in traditional juvenile justice philosophy is the ideal of individualized justice—that is, the assertion that each juvenile should be appraised and treated according to individual needs. To implement this ideal, court personnel have been granted vast discretionary power in order to diagnose and meet the needs of juveniles. Court personnel are invested with this power, not by default, but by design: They are charged with the awesome responsibility of evaluating a juvenile's entire life situation and offering a prognosis for the future.

A significant characteristic of traditional juvenile justice philosophy is that the situation and personal characteristics of the juvenile are consequential. The primary task of the juvenile court is to assess a juvenile's social situation, diagnose potential needs, and provide rehabilitative treatment if the child is viewed as requiring guidance or protection.

It is totally consistent with this orientation that a juvenile's characteristics, as perceived and interpreted by court personnel, be the most crucial variables in the decision making. Legal variables are important, but primarily as "symptoms" used by court personnel to evaluate other dimensions of a juvenile's life situation.

Critics suggest that, in contrast to the ideal of individualized justice in which each child is treated on the basis of particularized needs, the exercise of discretion in juvenile courts is more often based on stereotypical conceptions of societal subgroups. Opponents of juvenile justice system practices assert that, rather than being dealt with on an individual basis, youths are categorized and processed according to race and social class. Accordingly, critics suggest that minority and poor juveniles have been subjected to widespread, systematic discrimination.

The juvenile court's discretionary power, coupled with the pervasiveness of racial discrimination in American institutions, presents a potentially ominous situation for black youths who are brought before juvenile court. Juvenile justice researchers have, with varying degrees of success, sought to determine the nature and extent of racial discrimination in juvenile courts. A clear distinction exists between earlier work and more recent research. Characterized by sophisticated methodologies and a more encompassing conceptualization of process, recent research has provided a more specific and thorough depiction of justice decision making. Much of the earlier, pioneering work evidenced two major deficiencies: the oversimplification of process by focusing exclusively on single decision-making states; and the creation and perpetuation of an untenable dichotomy between legal and extralegal variables.

Most early work dealt with only one phase of the decision-making process. Many studies concentrated on the final disposition of the case (treatment or sentencing), while others focused on the detention decision (the decision whether or not to detain a juvenile prior to adjudication) or the screening decision (the decision whether to handle a case in a formal or informal manner). A few notable studies examined several junctures in the process, but did not explore the interplay between these decisions. Essentially, most research failed to examine the impact early decisions and professional judgments have on subsequent decisions. Recent research has demonstrated that such an emphasis on one decision, without attention to its impact on other junctures in the process, can create a misleading portrayal of decision making within the justice system (Farrell & Swigert, 1978; Liska & Tausig, 1979).

A further shortcoming of early research was the assumed distinction between legal process, and social (extralegal) variables—a construction that ignored interrelatedness of these factors. Those factors categorized as legal variables (offense type and prior record) and process variables (detention decision and screening decision) were often viewed as more objective criteria for decision making, as well as ex post facto indicators of a lack of bias. More recent research has provided critical insight into the role that social characteristics play in the original determination of legal variables and process variables (Hagan, Hewitt, & Alwin, 1979). The influence of race, and class or gender, may be most evident in initial stages of the juvenile court process (detention decision or screening decision); yet as a juvenile becomes increasingly enmeshed in the judicial system the impact of social characteristics is incorporated into the newly defined process variables. Early decision outcomes, in short, impact subsequent decisions. Bias is incorporated into initial legal decisions, and final disposition, the most commonly examined decision, is the last juncture and the point at which social characteristics are masked by prior process decisions (Dannefer & Schutt, 1982).

Two recent studies (Reed, 1984; Bortner & Reed, 1985) focused on juvenile court decision making as a multiphased process. They examined the contention that juvenile social characteristics (specifically race) greatly influence major early court decisions and that those decisions are influential indicators of final disposition, the last point in the decision-making process. Two major court decisions, in addition to severity of final disposition, were included in the model: detention decision and manner of handling (screening decision). The model also included two legal variables: offense type and prior record. Even with offense type and prior record taken into consideration (i.e., statistically controlled), the study found that black youths received more severe dispositions than white youths. Black youths were also much more likely to be detained prior to a hearing and were slightly more likely to be handled formally. The importance of this latter finding is that youths who are detained as well as those who are handled formally generally receive more severe dispositions. Thus, early juvenile court decisions predispose black youths to more severe final dispositions.

Any initial contact with the juvenile justice system for black youths may lead to more severe treatment. This in turn increases their chances for being differentially treated at the various decision-making points should there be any later involvement with the system.

Given both the discretionary powers of police officers in determining whether to take juvenile offenders into custody and the lingering existence of racial bias in police departments, racially different treatment could very well begin at the point of initial contact. In this way the social characteristics (i.e., race) of youths may get transformed into legal variables. Both sets of factors—social and legal—then act together and independently to affect the treatment of black youths in the juvenile justice system.

Since black youths are treated more harshly in the juvenile justice system than white youths, and since some officials of this system enjoy broad discretionary powers, it seems desirable to sensitize these officials and those who work with them (or who oversee the system) to the damaging effects that conscious or unconscious racial attitudes can have on black youths in the system. Similarly, it is important for these officials to understand the long-term adverse consequences that this situation has on the black community as a whole, as well as on the larger society.

The juvenile justice system has had a major negative impact on African-American youth. The increased detention of black youth in correctional facilities over the last three decades has had a severe negative impact on their chances for reasonable employment in our society (Hawkins & Jones, 1988). As shown above, black youth between the ages of 15 and 24 are disproportionately represented in juvenile and then adult correctional institutions. For most young people in this country this period of life is traditionally devoted to thinking about the future—attending college, choosing a profession, getting married, and so on. For many black youth, these options are not a functional part of planning life. Instead, youth who number among the disproportionately large number of black youth who become involved in the juvenile justice system obtain "marks" on their records that affect the type of job they may be considered for. This process also helps to create the situation described in recent research on the availability of marriageable black males, and their being able and capable of supporting a family (Wilson, 1987; Berlin & Sum, 1986).

CRIME, DRUGS, AND RACE

In any assessment of African-Americans and the criminal justice system the issues of crime and drugs, and their associations with race, demand attention. Though seldom stated, the disproportionate number of African-Americans in the criminal justice system raises issues of genetics, that is, "blacks may be genetically predisposed to crime." We address that issue below, as well as the issue of drugs and race, as an increasing proportion of inmate populations is African-American males incarcerated for illegal drug activity.

Crime and Race

The crime and criminal record statistics of African-Americans are alarming; and they keep getting worse. Blacks represent 12% of the population of the United States, yet

- 40% of death row inmates are black (Horton & Smith, 1990);
- 49, or 42%, of persons executed in the 1980s were black (Garwood, 1991);
- Blacks are 42% of the jail population (Horton & Smith, 1990) and 49% of the state and federal prison population (Garwood, 1992);
- Blacks are 28.9% of arrestees (Garwood, 1992);
- Blacks are 49% of all murder and nonnegligent homicide victims (Garwood, 1991);
- Black males in the United States are incarcerated at a rate four times higher than black males in South Africa, 3,109 per 100,000 in the population compared to 729 (Hoskins, 1991); and
- In 1986, the total number of black men of all ages in college was 426,000, while the number of young black men between the ages of 20 and 29 under the control of the criminal justice system (incarcerated, on parole, or on probation) was 609,690 (Hoskins, 1991).

These figures, of course, give us pause. Yet, it must be kept in mind that none of these figures demonstrates that blacks as a race are more prone to crime. Rather, the figures indicate that the average black person in the United States is more likely than the average white person to be so situated in the social structure that he or she is more likely to be involved in crime—and as discussed above, with an even higher likelihood of being arrested, convicted, and imprisoned.

For persons who tend to assume that the relatively high rate of black participation in the criminal justice system is because of nature, or genetics, instead of the social environment, or social conditions, an arithmetic exercise may be instructive. Korn and McCorkle (1959) reminded us that such racial determinism must take into consideration racial mixture:

> [A]ny valid racial study of criminality should apportion the criminality of these [racially mixed] groups under both white and Negro categories. Thus, in figuring the totals of white and Negro offenders, unmixed whites and unmixed Negroes would count as one (1.0) for each racial category; every person seven-eighths white would add 0.875 to the white and 0.125 to the Negro categories; each person three-quarters while would add 0.75 to the white and 0.25 to the Negro categories; the equally mixed, 0.5 to each category, etc. (p. 231)

Melville Herskovits (1930) estimated that of all persons classified as Negro, almost 15% were more white than black, approximately 25% were equally white and black, approximately 32% were more black than white, and approximately 6% were black mixed with Indian, leaving about 22% as unmixed. Herskovits thus concluded that about 40% of persons classified as blacks are more white than black or at least half-white, which led Korn and McCorkle (1959) to suggest that almost 40% of offenders contributing to the total of "Negro" crime are either half or more than half white, and that offenders would have the effect of redistributing a very considerable number of criminals from the black to the white side of the ledger.

Of course it is evident that we cannot determine the accuracy of such estimations of racial mixture. The point is, however, that such a simplistic exercise should force attention away from considerations of racial determinism as an explanation for the differentials in crime statistics and toward examinations of social factors—community dynamics as well as social structure. It should be clear that cultural, experiential, and other environmental factors are relevant. Such factors, of course, include antiblack bias by the community, the police, prosecutors, judges and juries.

Table 4.2
Percentage of Illicit Drug Use by Age, Sex, and Race

Age/Sex	Any Illicit Drug Use, Ever White	Any Illicit Drug Use, Ever Black	Cocaine Use, Ever White	Cocaine Use, Ever Black
Total	37.8	37.2	12.4	9.9
Male	42.4	44.5	16.0	14.8
Female	33.6	31.0	9.0	5.7
12-17 years	30.7	24.4	5.1	2.9
Male	31.2	28.7	6.2	4.5
Female	30.3	20.1	4.0	1.2
18-25 years	69.1	55.1	28.3	13.4
Male	68.6	62.1	31.8	16.3
Female	69.5	49.0	24.8	11.0
26-34 years	65.9	56.3	27.0	17.2
Male	73.8	61.4	33.3	23.5
Female	58.2	52.0	20.9	11.7
35+ years	20.3	25.2	4.0	7.6
Male	24.9	34.5	6.8	14.1
Female	16.4	17.9	1.6	2.4

Source: National Institute of Drug Abuse (1986). *1985 National Household Survey on Drug Abuse: Population Estimates.* Washington, DC: Author.

Blacks are also seen as being disproportionately involved in drugs. A common image of black urban communities is that they are places of high crime and illegal drug activity. Daily media reports propagate—if not create—this image, because most of the individuals covered in these activities in the news media are black. Data shown in Tables 4.2 and 4.3 indicate quite clearly that there is a significant difference between the actual criminal activity of blacks—especially drug use—and public perception.

Table 4.2 for instance, shows that black males do not differ very much from white males in overall illicit drug use; nor do black females differ much from white females. Whites, in fact, have a higher rate of illegal drug use than blacks until the age of 35. After the age of 35 black rates exceed white rates. The same comparisons obtain in the use of cocaine specifically. And as Table 4.3 exhibits, white high school students also use drugs at higher rates than do black students. Only with heroin use does black student use exceed the reported use by white students.

Table 4.3
Lifetime, Annual, and 30-Day Prevalence of Drug Use by Race, High School Senior Class of 1988

	Race	
	White	Black
Approximate Weighted N:	11,000	2,000
Marijuana/Hashish		
Lifetime	49.9%	36.6%
Annual	36.2	19.7
30-Day	19.9	9.8
Inhalants		
Lifetime	18.5	8.4
Annual	7.5	2.9
30-Day	2.9	1.8
Cocaine		
Lifetime	12.8	6.4
Annual	8.4	8.4
30-Day	3.7	1.4
"Crack"		
Lifetime	4.8	3.4
Annual	3.1	2.6
30-Day	1.5	1.3
Other Cocaine		
Lifetime	12.8	5.2
Annual	7.8	2.1
30-Day	3.2	1.5
Heroin		
Lifetime	1.1	1.4
Annual	0.4	0.8
30-Day	0.2	0.5
Alcohol		
Lifetime	94.2	84.4
Annual	89.0	69.9
30-Day	69.5	40.9
Cigarettes		
Lifetime	68.9	54.3
30-Day	32.3	12.8

Source: National Institute of Drug Abuse (1989). *Drug Abuse Among Racial/Ethnic Minorities.* Washington, DC: Author.

These illegal drug use data contrast sharply with both the image consistently put forth by media reports and with the apparent activity of law enforcement officials, each of which appears to focus on blacks and black communities. Since whites use illegal drugs at least as much as blacks and since there are nearly seven times (6.7) more whites than blacks in the country, an equitable distribution of images of drug users in the media would dictate up to six to seven times more whites than blacks.

These illegal drug use data shown in Tables 4.2 and 4.3 also contrast sharply with the racial distribution of jailed drug offenders. Nearly one-half of inmates in jail for drug offenses in the United States in 1989 were black (48.3%), compared to 25.5% white (Harlow, 1991). Some of this disparity is undoubtedly a function of the manner and place of drug activity in black communities. It appears that a significant proportion of both drug sales and use among blacks occurs in the streets and in areas with other crime problems—a situation that draws police attention. However, it does not seem plausible that these factors could produce the racial disparities that we see in arrests and incarceration for illegal drug activity.

CONCLUSION

The criminal justice system touches the lives of African-Americans more often than it does the lives of white Americans. Blacks tend to come in contact with the system more often than whites, whether that contact is a visit to see a relative or friend in prison or jail, or a stop by the police on certain suspicions. These contacts help mold the attitudes and perceptions that African-Americans hold about how the system operates. As the National Minority Advisory Council on Criminal Justice (NMAC) discovered in field hearings, blacks believe that they are singled out for punishment by the justice system "just for being black and poor" (1982). The NMAC report asserts that, to a significant degree, problems involving crime among blacks can be related to their economic status—for example, unemployment and underemployment—which causes frustration, despair, and hopelessness. This position is supported in the 1985 update of the National Commission on the Causes and Prevention of Violence in a section entitled "Black Violence and Public Policy" (Comer, 1988, p. 69):

> When parents are able to meet basic family needs, identify with institutional leaders, and experience a sense of belonging, they are likely to be adequate child rearers and to promote the social, psychological, and moral development of their children to a level that enables them to cope as young people and adults and

reduces the likelihood of crime and violence to a minimal and manageable level in society.

There can be little doubt that African-Americans commit a disproportionate share of street crime and that social and economic factors play major roles in the production of this crime. To address this excess crime issue we must look at the social structure, especially as it relates to African-Americans. On the other hand, when the issue is the unequal treatment by the criminal justice system, then the criminal justice system itself must be examined.

REFERENCES

Albonetti, C. (1985). Sentencing: The effects of uncertainty. Presented at the Law and Society Association meetings, San Diego.

Baab, G. W., & Furgeson, W. R., Jr., (1967). Texas sentencing practices: A statistical study. *Texas Law Review, 45*, 471.

Bachman, J. G., O'Malley, P. O., & Johnston, J. (1978). *Youth in transition: vol. VI. Adolescence to adulthood: Change and stability in the lives of young men.* Ann Arbor: University of Michigan, Institute of Social Research.

Baldus, D. C., Pulaski, C. A., & Woodworth, G. (1986). Arbitrariness and discrimination in the administration of the death penalty: A challenge to state supreme courts. *Stetson Law Review, 15*, 133–261.

Baldus, D. C., Woodworth, G., & Pulaski, C. A. (1985). Monitoring and evaluating contemporary death sentencing systems: Lessons from Georgia. *University of California–Davis Law Review, 18*, 1375–1407.

Baldus, D. C., Woodworth, G. C., & Pulaski, C. A. (1990). *Equal justice and the death penalty: A legal and empirical analysis.* Boston: Northeastern University Press.

Berlin, G., & Sum, A. (1986). American standards of living, family welfare and the basic skills crisis. Paper based on speech delivered by Gordon Berlin, in December 1986, at Conference of School and Employment and Training Officials, sponsored by the National Governors Association and the Chief State School Officers.

Bernstein, I., Kick, E., Leung, J., & Schultz, B. (1977). Charge reduction. *Social Forces, 56*, 362–384.

Blumstein, A. (1982). On the racial disproportionality of United States prison population. *Journal of Criminal Law and Criminology, 73*, 1259–1281.

Bortner, M. A., & Reed, W. L. (1985). The preeminence of process: An example of refocussed justice research. *Social Science Quarterly, 66* (1), 413–425.

Bowers, W. J. (1984). *Legal homicide: Death as punishment in America, 1864–1982.* Boston: Northeastern University Press.

Bowers, W. J., & Pierce, G. L. (1980). Arbitrariness and discrimination under post-Furman capital statutes. *Crime and Delinquency, 26*, 563–635.

Burke, P. J., & Turk, A. T. (1975). Factors affecting post-arrest decisions: A model for analysis. *Social Problems, 22*, 313.

Chiricos, G., & Waldo, P. (1975). Socioeconomic status and criminal sentencing: An empirical assessment of a conflict proposition. *American Sociological Review, 40*, 753–772.

Christianson, S. (1980). Racial discrimination and prison confinement—A follow-up. *Criminal Law Bulletin 16*, 616–621.

Clarke, S. H., & Koch, G. G. (1976). The influence of income and other factors on whether criminal defendants go to prison. *Law & Society Review, 11*, 57–92.

Coker v. Georgia, 433 U.S. 485 (1977).

Comer, J. (1988). Black violence and public policy. In L. A. Curtiss (Ed.), *American Violence and Public Policy*. New Haven: Yale University Press.

Cook, B. (1973). Sentencing behavior of federal judges: Draft cases–1972. *University of Cincinnati Law Review 42*, 597–633.

Dannefer, D., & Schutt, R. (1982). Race and juvenile justice processing in court and police agencies. *American Journal of Sociology, 87*, 1113–1132.

Eisenstein, J., & Jacob, H. (1977). *Felony justice: An organizational analysis of criminal courts*. Boston: Little, Brown.

Engle, C. D. (1971). *Criminal justice in the city: A study of sentence severity and variation in the Philadelphia criminal court system*. Ph.D. Dissertation, Temple University.

Farrell, A., & Swigert, V. L. (1978). Prior offense record as a self-fulfilling prophecy. *Law & Society Review, 12*, 437.

Furman v. Georgia, 408 U.S. 238 (1972).

Garwood, A. N. (1991). *Black Americans: A statistical sourcebook*. Boulder, CO: Number and Concepts.

Garwood, A. N. (1992). *Black Americans: A statistical sourcebook*. Boulder, CO: Number and Concepts.

Gibson, L. (1978). Race as a determinant of criminal sentences: A methodological critique and a case study. *Law & Society Review, 12*, 455–478.

Gold, M., & Reimer, D. J. (1975). Changing patterns of delinquent behavior among Americans 13–16 years old—1972. *Crime and Delinquency Literature, 7*, 483–517.

Greenfield, L. A. (1992). Capital punishment, 1990. *Bureau of Justice Statistics Bulletin*. Washington, DC: U.S. Department of Justice.

Greenwood, P. C., Wildhorn, S., Poggio, E. C., Strumwasser, M. J., & DeLeon, P. (1973). *Prosecution of adult felony defendants in Los Angeles county: A police perspective*. Santa Monica: Rand.

Gregg v. Georgia, 96 S. Ct. 2950 (1976).

Gross, S. R., & Mauro, R. (1984). Patterns of death: An analysis of racial disparities and homicide victimization. *Stanford Law Review, 37*, 27–153.

Gruhl, J., Welch, S., & Spohn, C. (1984). Women as criminal defendants: A test for paternalism. *Western Political Quarterly, 37*, 456–467.

Hagan, J. (1974). Extra-legal attributes and criminal sentencing: An assessment of a sociological viewpoint. *Law and Society Review, 8*, 357–383.

Hagan, J., & Bumiller, K. (1983). Making sense of sentencing: A review and critique of sentencing research. In A. Blumstein, J. Cohen, S. Martin, & M. Tonny (Eds.), *Research on Sentencing: The Search for Reform*, Vol. II. Washington, DC: National Academy Press.

Hagan, J., Hewitt, K., & Alwin, D. (1979). Ceremonial justice. *Social Forces, 58*, 506–527.

Harlow, C. W. (1991). Drugs and jail inmates, 1989. *Bureau of Justice Statistics Special Report*. Washington, DC: U.S. Department of Justice.

Hawkins, D. F., & Jones, N. (1988). Black adolescents and the criminal justice system. In R. L. Jones (Ed.), *Black Adolescents*. Berkeley, CA: Cobbard Henry.

Herskovits, M. J. (1930). *The anthropometry of the American Negro*. New York: Columbia University Press.

Horton, C. P., & Smith, J. C. (1990). *Statistical record of black America*. New York: Gale Research.

Hoskins, L. A. (Ed.). (1991, April). *Newsletter*. Volume XV, Number 3. Kent, OH: Kent State University, Institute for African American Affairs.

Huizinga, D., & Elliott, D. S. (1987). Juvenile offenders: prevalence, offender incidence and arrest rates by race. *Crime and Delinquency, 33*, 206–223.

Institute for Public Policy and Management. (1986). *Racial and ethnic disparities in imprisonment*. Seattle: University of Washington.

Jacoby, J. E., & Paternoster, R. (1982). Sentencing disparity and jury packing: Further challenge to the death penalty. *Journal of Criminal Law and Criminology, 73*, 379–387.

Jurek v. Texas, 96 S. Ct. 2950 (1976).

Kleck, G. (1981). Racial discrimination in criminal sentencing: A critical evaluation of the evidence with additional evidence on the death penalty. *American Sociological Review, 46*, 783–804.

Korn, R. R., & McCorkle, L. W. (1959). *Criminology and penology*. New York: Holt, Rinehart and Winston.

Krisberg, B., Schwartz, I., Fishman, G., Eisikovits, Z., Guttman, E., & Joe, K. (1987). The incarceration of minority youth. *Crime and Delinquency, 33*, 173–205.

LaFree, G. D. (1980). Variables affecting guilty pleas and convictions in rape cases: Toward a social theory of rape processing. *Social Forces, 58*, 833–850.

LaFree, G. D. (1985). Official reactions to Hispanic defendants in the southwest. *Journal of Research in Crime and Delinquency, 22*, 213–237.

Levin, A. (1977). *Urban politics and criminal courts*. Chicago: University of Chicago Press.

Lewis, A. (April 28, 1987). Making inequity acceptable. *The New York Times.*

Liska, E., & Tausig, M. (1979). Theoretical interpretations of social class and racial differentials in legal decision-making for juveniles. *Sociological Quarterly, 20*, 197–207.

Lizotte, A. J. (1978). Extra-legal factors in Chicago's criminal courts: Testing the conflict model of criminal justice, *Social Problems, 25*, 564–580.

Lotz, R., & Hewitt, J. D. (1977). The influence of legally irrelevant factors on felony sentencing. *Sociological Inquiry, 47*, 39–48.

McCleskey, v. Kemp, 107 S. Ct. 1756 (1987).

Myers, M. A. (1979). Offended parties and official reactions: Victims and the sentencing of criminal defendants. *Sociological Quarterly, 20*, 529–540.

NAACP Legal Defense Fund. (1992, Summer). *Death row, U.S.A.* Unpublished compilation.

National Institute of Drug Abuse (1986). *1985 National household survey on drug abuse: Population estimates.* Washington, DC: Author.

National Institute of Drug Abuse (1989). *Drug abuse among racial/ethnic minorities.* Washington, DC: Author.

National Minority Advisory Council on Criminal Justice. (1982). The inequality of justice: A report on crime and the administration of justice in the minority community. Washington, DC: U.S. Department of Justice.

The New York Times. (April 24, 1987).

Paternoster, R. (1984). Prosecutorial discretion in requesting the death penalty: A case of victim-based racial discrimination. *Law and Society Review, 18*, 437–478.

Petersilia, J. (1983). *Racial disparities in the criminal justice system.* Santa Monica, CA: Rand.

Pope, C.E. (1975). *Sentencing of California felony offenders.* Washington, DC: U.S. Department of Justice, Law Enforcement Assistance Administration, Criminal Justice Research Center.

Profitt v. Florida, 96 S. Ct. 2960 (1976).

Radelet, M. L. (1981). Racial characteristics and the imposition of the death penalty. *American Sociological Review, 46*, 918–927.

Radelet, M. L. (1985). Rejecting the jury: The imposition of the death penalty in Florida. *University of California–Davis Law Review, 18*, 1409–1431.

Radelet, M. L. (1989). Executions of whites for crimes against blacks: Exceptions to the rule? *Sociological Quarterly, 30*, 529–544.

Radelet, M.L., & Mello, M. (1986). Executing those who kill blacks: An unusual case study. *Mercer Law Review, 37*, 911–925.

Radelet, M. L., & Pierce, G. L. (1985). Race and prosecutorial discretion in homicide cases. *Law and Society Review, 19*, 587–621.

Radelet, M. L., & Vandiver, M. (1986). Racial and capital punishment: An overview of the issues. *Crime and Social Justice, 25*, 94–114.

Reed, W. L. (1984). *Racial differentials in juvenile court processing* (IUR Research Report #8). Baltimore: Morgan State University, Institute for Urban Research.

Reed, W. L. (1991). Trends in homicide among African-Americans. *Trotter Institute Review, 5*(3), 11–18.

Roberts v. Louisiana, 96 S. Ct. 3001 (1976).

Sigler, R., & Horn, M. (1986). Race, income and penetration of the justice system. *Criminal Justice Review, 11*, 1–8.

Spohn, C., Welch, S., & Gruhl, J. (1981). Women defendants in court: The interaction between sex and race in convicting and sentencing. *Social Science Quarterly, 66*, 178–185.

Sutton, L. P. (1978a). *Federal sentencing patterns: A study of geographical variations.* Albany, NY: Criminal Justice Research Center.

Sutton, L. P. (1978b). *Variations in federal criminal sentences: A statistical assessment at the national level.* Albany, NY: Criminal Justice Research Center.

Tiffany, L. P., Avichal, Y., & Peters, G. W. (1975). A statistical analysis of sentencing in federal courts: Defendants convicted after trial, 1967–1968. *Journal of Legal Studies, 4*, 369–390.

Uhlman, T. M. (1977). The impact of defendant race in trial court sentencing decisions. In J. A. Gardiner (Ed.), *Public Law and Public Policy*. New York: Praeger.

U.S. Department of Justice. 1980. *Capital punishment—1980*. Washington, DC: Government Printing Office.

Unnever, J., Frazier, C., & Heneretta, J. (1980). Race differences in criminal sentencing. *Sociological Quarterly, 21*, 197–206.

Welch, S., & Combs, M. (1985). Intra-racial differences in attitudes of blacks: Class cleavages or consensus? *Phylon, 46*, 91–97.

Welch, S., Spohn, C., & Gruhl, J. (1984). Dismissal, conviction and incarceration of Hispanic defendants: A comparison with blacks and Anglos. *Social Science Quarterly, 65* (June), 265–277.

Welch, S., Spohn, C., & Gruhl, J. (1985). Convicting and sentencing differences among black, Hispanic, and white males in six localities. *Justice Quarterly, 2* (March), 67–80.

Wicker, T. (April 28, 1987). *Bowing to racism. The New York Times.*

Wilson, W. J. (1987). *The truly disadvantaged: The inner city, the under class and public policy.* Chicago: University of Chicago Press.

Wolfgang, M. E., & Reidel, M. (1977). Race, judicial discretion and the death penalty. *Annals of the American Academy of Political and Social Science, 53*, 301–311.

Woodson v. North Carolina, 96 S. Ct. 2979 (1976).

Worton, S. M. (1977). *Law enforcement and justice*. Rochelle Park, NJ: Hayden Book Co.

Zatz, M. (1984). Race, ethnicity and determinate sentencing. *Criminology, 22* (May), 147–171.

Appendix: Assessment of the Status of African-Americans, Project Study Group Members and Contributors

PROJECT LEADERS

Director: Wornie L. Reed, William Monroe Trotter Institute, University of Massachusetts at Boston, 1985–1991 (since August 1991, Urban Child Research Center, Cleveland State University)

Co-Chair: James E. Blackwell, Department of Sociology, University of Massachusetts at Boston

Co-Chair: Lucius J. Barker, Department of Political Science, Washington University

STUDY GROUP ON EDUCATION

Charles V. Willie (Chair), School of Education, Harvard University

Antoine M. Garibaldi (Vice-Chair), Dean, College of Arts and Science, Xavier University

Robert A. Dentler, Department of Sociology, University of Massachusetts at Boston

Robert C. Johnson, Minority Studies Academic Program, St. Cloud State University

Meyer Weinberg, Department of Education, University of Massachusetts at Amherst

STUDY GROUP ON EMPLOYMENT, INCOME, AND OCCUPATIONS

William Darity, Jr. (Chair), Department of Economics, University of North Carolina at Chapel Hill

Barbara Jones (Vice-Chair), College of Business, Prairie View A&M University

Jeremiah P. Cotton, Department of Economics, University of Massachusetts at Boston

Herbert Hill, Industrial Relations Research Institute, University of Wisconsin

STUDY GROUP ON POLITICAL PARTICIPATION AND THE ADMINISTRATION OF JUSTICE

Michael B. Preston (Chair), Department of Political Science, University of Southern California

Dianne M. Pinderhughes (Vice-Chair), Department of Political Science, University of Illinois–Champaign

Tobe Johnson, Department of Political Science, Morehouse College

Nolan Jones, Committee on Criminal Justice and Public Protection, National Governors Association

Susan Welch, Department of Political Science, University of Nebraska

John Zipp, Department of Sociology, University of Wisconsin at Milwaukee

STUDY GROUP ON SOCIAL AND CULTURAL CHANGE

Alphonso Pinkney (Chair), Department of Sociology, Hunter College

James Turner (Vice-Chair), African Studies and Research Center, Cornell University

John Henrik Clarke, Professor Emeritus, Department of Black and Puerto Rican Studies, Hunter College

Sidney Wilhelm, Department of Sociology, State University of New York–Buffalo

STUDY GROUP ON HEALTH STATUS AND MEDICAL CARE

William Darity, Sr. (Chair), School of Public Health, University of Massachusetts at Amherst

Stanford Roman (Vice-Chair), Morehouse School of Medicine, Atlanta

Claudia Baquet, National Cancer Institute, Bethesda, Maryland

Noma L. Roberson, Department of Cancer Control and Epidemiology, Roswell Park Cancer Institute, Buffalo, NY

STUDY GROUP ON THE FAMILY

Robert B. Hill (Chair), Institute for Urban Research, Morgan State University

Andrew Billingsley (Vice-Chair), Department of Family and Community Development, University of Maryland
Eleanor Engram, Engram-Miller Associates, Cleveland, Ohio
Michelene R. Malson, Department of Public Policy Studies, Duke University
Roger H. Rubin, Department of Family and Community Development, University of Maryland
Carol B. Stack, Social and Cultural Studies, Graduate School of Education, University of California at Berkeley
James B. Stewart, Black Studies Program, Pennsylvania State University
James E. Teele, Department of Sociology, Boston University

CONTRIBUTORS

Carolyne Arnold, College of Public and Community Services, University of Massachusetts at Boston
James Banks, School of Education, University of Washington
Margaret Beale Spencer, College of Education, Emory University
Bob Blauner, Department of Sociology, University of California at Berkeley
Larry Carter, Department of Sociology, University of Oregon
Obie Clayton, School of Criminal Justice, University of Nebraska
James P. Comer, Department of Psychiatry, Yale Medical School
Charles Flowers, Department of Education, Fisk University
Bennett Harrison, Urban Studies and Planning, Massachusetts Institute of Technology
Norris M. Haynes, Child Study Center, New Haven
Joseph Himes, Excellence Fund Professor Emeritus of Sociology, University of North Carolina at Greensboro
Hubert E. Jones, School of Social Work, Boston University
James M. Jones, Department of Psychology, University of Delaware
Faustine C. Jones-Wilson, *Journal of Negro Education*, Howard University
Barry A. Krisberg, National Council on Crime and Delinquency, San Francisco
Hubert G. Locke, Society of Justice Program, University of Washington
E. Yvonne Moss, William Monroe Trotter Institute, University of Massachusetts at Boston
Willie Pearson, Jr., Department of Sociology, Wake Forest University
Michael L. Radelet, Department of Sociology, University of Florida
Robert Rothman, *Education Week*, Washington, DC
Diana T. Slaughter, School of Education, Northwestern University

A. Wade Smith, Department of Sociology, Arizona State University
Leonard Stevens, Compact for Educational Opportunity, Milwaukee
Wilbur Watson, Geriatrics Department, Morehouse School of Medicine
Warren Whatley, Department of Economics, University of Michigan
John B. Williams, Graduate School of Education, Harvard University
Rhonda Williams, Afro-American Studies, University of Maryland
Reginald Wilson, American Council of Education, Washington, DC

Index

About the Contributors

ROY AUSTIN is associate professor of sociology at Pennsylvania State University where he has been a faculty member since 1972. He is a member of the American Sociological Association, the American Society of Criminology, and the Caribbean Studies Association. He has published extensively in criminology and sociological professional journals, and is currently involved in research on the death penalty and deterrence.

OBIE CLAYTON is presently director of the Morehouse Research Institute and associate professor of sociology at Morehouse College. He is also editor of *Challenge: A Journal of Research on African American Men*. Previously, he was on the faculty at the University of Nebraska at Omaha, Atlanta University, and the University of Massachusetts at Boston. He served as a member of the Evaluation Team of the Atlanta Project and is co-principal investigator of "The Atlanta Social Survey on Urban Inequality."

JEREMIAH P. COTTON is associate professor of economics at the University of Massachusetts at Boston, where he has been a member of the faculty since 1985. Prior to that he was on the faculty at North Carolina State University and the California State University at Fresno. He has published in many social science and political economy journals and his honors and awards include a Social Sciences Research Council doctoral fellowship.

WILLIAM DARITY, JR. is the Cary C. Boshamer Professor of Economics at the University of North Carolina at Chapel Hill. The central theme of his research is the question of inequality—between nations, between regions, between ethnic and racial groups, and between persons. He is the co-author of *The Loan Pushers*, a study of the role of the commercial banks in propagating the international debt crisis of the 1980s, as well as editor of four books.

HERBERT HILL is professor of Afro-American studies and industrial relations at the University of Wisconsin-Madison. He is the former National Labor Director of the NAACP and author of *Black Labor and the American Labor System*. He was a consultant to the Economic and Social Council of the United Nations and to the U.S. Equal Employment Opportunity Commission. He has presented testimony before congressional committees and frequently appears as an expert witness in federal employment discrimination litigation.

TOBE JOHNSON is chairman and professor of political science and director of urban studies at Morehouse College. Previously he was a faculty member of the Graduate School of Public and International Affairs at the University of Pittsburgh, Carleton College, and Prairie View College.

NOLAN JONES is the director for the Committee on Justice and Public Safety of the National Governors' Association. Previously, he was assistant professor of political science at the University of Michigan in Ann Arbor. He has conducted research and published articles in the areas of constitutional law, race relations, criminal justice, and public policy. He has published extensively in criminology and sociological professional journals. Currently, he serves as an adjunct professor of government at the American University in Washington, D.C.

BARRY A. KRISBERG is president of the National Council on Crime and Delinquency (NCCD), headquartered in San Francisco, California. He has been on the faculty at the University of Minnesota's Hubert Humphrey Institute of Public Affairs, and the University of California at Berkeley in both the Legal Studies Program and the School of Criminology. He has authored several publications in the area of juvenile justice and is a member of the International Society of Criminology and the National Association of Juvenile Correctional Administrators.

HUBERT G. LOCKE is professor and, from 1982-1988, was dean of the Graduate School of Public Affairs at the University of Washington where he was also director of the Program in Society and Justice. He was administrative assistant to the commissioner of police in Detroit (1966–1967), and the author of numerous works in the law and justice field including *The Detroit Riot of 1967*.

E. YVONNE MOSS is associate professor of politics at the University of San Francisco. Prior to that, she was research scientist at the William Monroe Trotter Institute at the University of Massachusetts in Boston. She has also been a faculty member at Southeastern Massachusetts University. Her research interests are urban politics, judicial politics, American politics, African-American and ethnic politics, and comparative politics.

DIANNE M. PINDERHUGHES is professor of political science and Afro-American studies and director of the Afro-American Studies and Research Program at the University of Illinois, Urbana-Champaign. She taught at Dartmouth College and was a visiting professor at Howard University before coming to the University of Illinois. Her book *Race and Ethnicity in Chicago Politics: A Reexamination of Pluralist Theory* was published in 1987. She has also published numerous articles and book reviews addressing issues of race and public policy.

ALPHONSO PINKNEY is professor emeritus of sociology, Hunter College, the City University of New York. He has been a professor of sociology at the University of Chicago (1969-1971), Howard University (1971-1972), and a professor of criminology at the University of California at Berkeley (1973-1975). His books include *Black Americans; The American Way of Violence; Red, Black and Green: Black Nationalism in the United States;* and *The Myth of Black Progress*.

MICHAEL B. PRESTON is currently professor and chair of the department of political science at the University of Southern California. Urban and black politics and public administration are his research interests. His books include *The New Black Politics*; *The Politics of Bureaucratic Reform; Race, Sex and Policy Problems;* and *Racial and Ethnic Politics in California*.

MICHAEL L. RADELET is professor of sociology, University of Florida. He completed two years of postdoctoral work in psychiatry at the University of Wisconsin before coming to the University of Florida in 1979. He has published four books and numerous papers in law, sociology, and criminology journals on various aspects of the death penalty.

WORNIE L. REED is currently professor of sociology and director of the Urban Child Research Center at Cleveland State University. Previously, he developed and directed the William Monroe Trotter Institute and chaired the Department of Black Studies at the University of Massachusetts and prior to that, he was director of the Institute of Urban Research at Morgan State University. While at the Trotter Institute he directed the Study on the Assessment of the Status of African Americans which resulted in this book as well as *The Education of African Americans* (1991), *Health and Medical Care of African Americans* (1993), and *Research on the African-American Family: A Holistic Perspective* (1993).

JAMES TURNER is founder of the Africana Studies and Research Center at Cornell University where he is a professor of political sociology and has been on the faculty since 1969. His research interests are focused in the areas of racial stratification, labor market participation, African American politics and public policy. He is active in the Association of Black Sociologists, the African Heritage Association, and the National Conference of Black Studies.

SUSAN WELCH is professor of political science and dean of the College of the Liberal Arts at Pennsylvania State University. She has also held faculty positions at the University of Nebraska and the University of Ottawa. Some of her recent books include *Black Americans' Views of Racial Inequality: The Dream Deferred; Urban Reform and Its Consequences: A Study in Representation;* and *Women: Elections and Representation.* She has served as president of the Midwest Political Science Association, treasurer of the American Political Science Association, and editor of *American Politics Quarterly.*

SIDNEY WILHELM is recently retired as professor of sociology at the State University of New York at Buffalo. Among his many publications is the book *Who Needs the Negro?*, first published in 1971.

JOHN F. ZIPP is currently associate professor of sociology and urban studies at the University of Wisconsin-Milwaukee. He is also coordinator of the university's Ph.D. program in Urban Studies and the associate director of its Center for Economic Development. His research has focused on political attitudes and behavior, especially the impact of class, race and gender; and the sociology of work and economic development.